W9-BBE-153

Prometheus Books

59 John Glenn Drive
Amherst, New York 14228-2197

THE ANNOTATED ANCIENT MARINER

With an Introduction and Notes by
MARTIN GARDNER

THE RIME
OF THE
ANCIENT MARINER

BY SAMUEL TAYLOR COLERIDGE

ILLUSTRATED BY GUSTAVE DORÉ

Published 2003 by Prometheus Books

Inquiries should be addressed to
Prometheus Books
59 John Glenn Drive
Amherst, New York 14228–2197
VOICE: 716–691–0133, ext. 207
FAX: 716–564–2711
WWW.PROMETHEUSBOOKS.COM

07 06 05 04 03   5 4 3 2 1

Library of Congress Cataloging-in-Publication Data

Coleridge, Samuel Taylor, 1772-1834.
   [Rime of the ancient mariner]
   The annotated ancient mariner. The rime of the ancient mariner / by Samuel Taylor Coleridge ; with an introduction and notes by Martin Gardner ; original illustrations by Gustave Doré. — 2nd ed.
      p. cm.
   Includes bibliographical references.
   ISBN 1-59102-125-1 (cloth : alk. paper)
   1. Animals—Treatment—Poetry. 2. Albatrosses—Poetry. 3. Antarctica—Poetry. 4. Aged men—Poetry. 5. Penance—Poetry. 6. Sailors—Poetry. I. Gardner, Martin, 1914– II. Doré, Gustave, 1832–1883. III. Title.

PR4479.A2G37 2003
821'.7—dc21

                                                          2003012747

Printed in Canada on acid-free paper

For my niece
Cynthia Anne Gardner

Contents

But I do not think "The Rime of the Ancient Mariner" was for Coleridge an escape from reality: I think it was reality, I think he was on the ship and made the voyage and felt and knew it all.

—THOMAS WOLFE,
in a letter of 1932, included in
The Letters of Thomas Wolfe,
edited by Elizabeth Nowell,
Charles Scribner's Sons, 1956, p. 322.

PREFACE
TO THE
Second Edition

This new edition of my *Annotated Ancient Mariner*, first published by Clarkson Potter in 1965 and long out of print, is little altered from the first edition. I have corrected a few errors, added to six footnotes, and written this new preface.

I make no apologies for the Doré illustrations. In 1965 there was little interest in Gustave Doré. Art critics and intellectuals dismissed him as little more than a popular illustrator of books and poems, not to be taken seriously as an artist. Since then tastes have changed. The current trend is a rediscovery of representational art. It's not easy to keep finding great artistic merit in, say, the meaningless dribblings of Jackson Pollock, the boring bicolored rectangles of Mark Rothko, or the thick black slashes of Franz Kline that manage to be uglier than a printed Chinese word.

Surely the great symbolic turning point was the November 2001 exhibit of Norman Rockwell at New York City's Guggenheim Museum. Rockwell at the Guggenheim! Who could have predicted it? Hard as it is for some to believe, today one can say kind words about Wyeth and Rockwell and even Doré without being thought a bumpkin of low aesthetic taste. The *New York Times Book Review*, on two full pages about the Rockwell show, was headed "Renaissance of a 'Lightweight.' " The *New Yorker* puzzled over Rockwell's unique "genius."

I have made no effort to enlarge my bibliography with the hundreds of books and articles about

Coleridge and Doré published since 1965. There are, however, two books I wish especially to recommend. One is the splendid two-volume biography of Coleridge by Richard Holmes, the last of which appeared in 1999. The other book is *Doré: Adrift on Dreams of Splendor*, by Doré collector Dan Malan, who published the book himself in 1995. It is the best-documented, best-illustrated, work on Doré yet to cover Doré's fantastic output. He was, of course, far and away the most popular and most prolific illustrator of all time.

In addition to a fine biography of Doré (I'll bet you didn't know that Sarah Bernhardt was one of Doré's many notable lovers), Malan catalogs more than ten thousand Doré engravings, five thousand books with his illustrations, thirty sculptures, and four hundred oil paintings in full color. Malan's bibliography is the most complete in print in any language, and the only catalog of such scope in English. The book is available only from the author, at 7518 Lindbergh Drive, St. Louis, MO 63117. His e-mail address is danmalan@aol.com.

—Martin Gardner

Introduction

The text of *The Rime of the Ancient Mariner,* in this newly annotated printing, is taken from the last edition of Coleridge's *Poetical Works* (1834) published in his lifetime. It is essentially the same as the text in *Sibylline Leaves* (1817). The poem's first version, in *Lyrical Ballads* (1798), is given after the 1834 version, with some additional notes on words, lines, and stanzas that Coleridge later excised. For the second edition of *Lyrical Ballads* (1800) Coleridge removed several dozen archaic words, took out forty-six lines, added seven. The marginal gloss and eighteen more lines were added to the *Sibylline Leaves* printing, and nine lines were deleted. Only trivial changes were made in later printings.

For the most part, the notes in this volume are intended to deepen the reader's understanding of the ballad as a straightforward narrative, without going into more general questions of symbolic and moral intent. Preceding the poem is a biograghical sketch of Coleridge which emphasizes those aspects of his many-sided life and personality that have the strongest bearing on the poem, especially on circumstances surrounding its composition. Following the poem, a chapter summarizes major critical attitudes toward the ballad, discusses possible higher levels of meaning, and closes with questions concerning the poem's much-debated moral. What sort of moral is it? What relevance can it have for us today?

Coleridgean scholars who may stoop to read this book are not likely to learn from it anything they do not already know. I cannot pretend to have done any sort of original work on the poem; indeed, more than half the notes could have been written by any careful, sympathetic reader of John Livingston Lowes's *The Road to Xanadu*. But *The Road to Xanadu* is a road of almost 600 pages, and even for readers who have studied Lowes, I believe a useful purpose is served by culling from it material that strengthens one's immediate understanding of the poem, and placing this information where it is readily accessible while the poem is actually being experienced.

I make no apologies for reproducing the Doré illustrations. They are something of a gamble, for Doré has been out of fashion for many decades. It is easy to speak of his "romantic realism" and "shallow virtuosity." It is also easy to forget that the first purpose of graphic illustrations for a narrative is graphically to illustrate the narrative. A good illustration should reinforce the mood of a text, as a good melody for a song should reinforce the mood of the lyrics. *The Ancient Mariner* is surely a work of romantic realism. It was Coleridge's explicit intent to write about the supernatural with the greatest possible verisimilitude, and to arouse in his readers that "willing suspension of disbelief" which he believed so essential to imaginative writing. Fantasy such as *The Ancient Mariner* demands, above all, realism on the part of any artist who attempts to illustrate it.

Moreover, I suspect (I may be wrong) that as much public hunger for representational art is slowly building up in the United States as hunger for non-representational art must be slowly building up in sophisticated circles of the Soviet Union. For half a century Western painters, annoyed by the growing role of photography in our culture, have been trying desperately to prove they could do all sorts of things a camera cannot do. The great joke has been that cameras are quite capable of producing non-objective art. It is much easier, for example, to take a color picture that resembles an action painting than to take a black-and-white photograph that resembles a Doré drawing. Coleridge, who had a keen eye for patterns and texture, once jotted down in a notebook an experiment in action art that would have made a splendid abstract photograph if color cameras had then been available. I quote from Humphry House's *Coleridge*:

> What a beautiful thing urine is, in a Pot, brown yellow, transpicuous, the Image diamond shaped of the Candle in it; especially as it now appeared, I having emptied the Snuffers into it & the Snuff floating about, & painting all-shaped Shadows on the Bottom.

Introduction

Now that abstract expressionism has abandoned the New York galleries for the professionally Pollocked walls of wealthy businessmen, there seems to be a stealthy creep of realism back into the galleries. By "realism" I do not mean Pop art, the so-called "new realism." (Who would have thought it possible to find a gimmick that would produce paintings uglier than, say, those clumps of black brush strokes by Franz Kline or more banal than those colored stripes of Mark Rothko?) Still, Pop art may be a straw in some sort of representational wind. Artistic taste, to a greater extent than most people will admit, is conditioned by simple boredom. Live for twenty years in a house dominated by the color pink and your eyes ache for any color *but* pink. To me, at any rate, Doré's crowded, romantic illustrations for *The Ancient Mariner*, first published in 1875 by the Doré Gallery in London, are a refreshing visual holiday.

The ballad has, of course, been admirably illustrated by scores of other artists, in wildly different styles. Surely the *worst* pictures ever bound together with the poem are Alexander Calder's, for an expensive volume published in 1946 by Reynal and Hitchcock. Admirers of Thomas Wolfe may recall that savage description in *You Can't Go Home Again* (Chap. 18, "Piggy Logan's Circus") of a Manhattan party at which Calder demonstrates his bent-wire circus puppets. This was before Calder had become famous for his dangling mobiles, but his puppets were then something of a rage in the city's *avant-garde* circles. Everybody at the party had to feign interest when, in truth, they were bewildered and annoyed. I mention this because I once had a strangely similar experience at the University of Chicago. The campus poetry society had arranged an exhibition of the originals of Calder's *Ancient Mariner* illustrations. We all stood around sipping tea and trying to think of something to say about what was hanging on the walls. For reasons best known to himself, Calder had drawn, in wiggly black lines, the Mariner and all his shipmates as stark naked figures with dangling phalli. In those days I suppose the pictures had a mild shock value; today they seem merely silly, like gay imitations of Thurber cartoons.

Later, when I had the big book itself in my hands, I turned the pages eagerly to see how Calder had handled that picturesque scene in Part III where the black skeleton of Death and his red-lipped harlot cast dice for the Mariner's soul. The harlot, for all we know from Coleridge's text, may actually have been nude; she is so portrayed by many illustrators. Alas, there was no such scene. Either it was too much for

Calder's talents, or he had no plausible excuse for attaching male sex organs to either figure.

I would like to express my gratitude to Norman Charles Brennan, of Niagara University, for reading the manuscript of this book and offering innumerable suggestions of great value, and to LaVere Anderson, of Tulsa, for calling my attention to the references to Coleridge in Thomas Wolfe's letters. To Harper & Row Publishers, Inc., I am indebted for permission to reprint "The Albatross" by Charles Baudelaire, from *Flowers of Evil,* translated by George Dillon and Edna St. Vincent Millay (copyright 1936 by George Dillon and Edna St. Vincent Millay, copyright © 1962 by George Dillon). As always, my wife helped in many ways.

MARTIN GARDNER
HASTINGS-ON-HUDSON, N. Y.

PART   I

Samuel Taylor Coleridge

The Albatross

Sometimes, to entertain themselves, the men of the crew
Lure upon deck an unlucky albatross, one of those vast
Birds of the sea that follow unwearied the voyage through,
Flying in slow and elegant circles above the mast.

No sooner have they disentangled him from their nets
Than this aërial colossus, shorn of his pride,
Goes hobbling pitiably across the planks and lets
His great wings hang like heavy, useless oars at his side.

How droll is the poor floundering creature, how limp and
    weak—
He, but a moment past so lordly, flying in state!
They tease him: One of them tries to stick a pipe in his
    beak;
Another mimics with laughter his odd lurching gait.

The Poet is like that wild inheritor of the cloud,
A rider of storms, above the range of arrows and slings;
Exiled on earth, at bay amid the jeering crowd,
He cannot walk for his unmanageable wings.

Charles Baudelaire,
translated by George Dillon.

1. Coleridge probably pronounced his name with a long "o" and in two syllables, as indicated by the following lines from one of his poems:

> Could you stand upon Skiddaw,
> you would not from the whole ridge
> See a man who so loves you as
> your fond S. T. COLERIDGE.

But, as John Livingston Lowes points out (*The Road to Xanadu*, Chap. XVIII, Note 35), Coleridge also wrote this epigram:

> Parry seeks the Polar ridge,
> Rhymes seeks S. T. Coleridge;

And these lines:

> Elsewhere in College, knowledge,
> wit and scholarage
> To Friends and Public known as
> S. T. Coleridge.

A fourth possibility is that, as a joke, the poet rhymed his name incorrectly in all three instances, and that the correct pronunciation rhymes with "doll ridge."

Samuel Taylor Coleridge

When young Charles Baudelaire finished his education in Paris, his guardians packed him off on an ocean voyage that carried him around the Cape. Observing sailors trap albatrosses for sport, he was struck by the contrast between the majestic beauty of these birds, flying high above the ship, and their pathetic, lurching gait on the ship's deck. Years later, in *Flowers of Evil,* this cruelty furnished the theme for one of his most memorable poems. I do not know if Baudelaire had Coleridge in mind when he likened the albatross to the poet, but it would be hard to find a more appropriate metaphor for the soaring beauty of Coleridge's imagination and his awkward, comic, painful flounderings across the planks of the earth.

Samuel Taylor Coleridge[1] was born October 21, 1772, at Ottery St. Mary, Devonshire, England. His father, a friendly, absent-minded vicar and schoolmaster, had four children by his first wife, ten by his second. Samuel was the youngest. He was a dreamy, precocious child who hated physical sports (though later in life he enjoyed swimming and mountain climbing) and whose time was occupied mostly in reading every book he could get his hands on.

When his father died (Coleridge was then ten), his mother sent him to London to complete his early schooling at Christ's Hospital, a famous charitable institution known as the Blue-coat School. Each boy wore a long, blue gown, knee-britches, yellow petticoat, yellow stockings, blue cap. "He seldom had two garters at one time," a schoolmate of Coleridge's later recalled, "in consequence of which his stockings used to drop into a series of not very elegant folds." Another schoolfellow remembered his habit of strolling about the yard reciting Greek verse. Coleridge and Charles Lamb, a student two years his junior, became lifelong friends.

It was at Christ's Hospital that young Coleridge discovered *Sonnets on Picturesque Spots* by the Reverend William Lisle Bowles. Today, Bowles's poetry seems bland and uninspired, but at the time it was something of a tradition-breaker. Coleridge later declared that Bowles was the first poet he had ever read who spoke of nature in a simple, natural diction. Too poor to buy more copies, Coleridge actually transcribed Bowles's entire book more than forty times so he could give out copies to friends! He himself began to feel the Muse's inspiration. An early sonnet pays generous tribute to Bowles, though it begins with what is surely one of the least promising opening phrases in English poetry: "My heart has thank'd thee, Bowles!"

Coleridge was 19 when he left London to accept a scholarship at Jesus College, Cambridge. For a short time he took his studies seriously, but soon was reading everything except what he was supposed to read. His mind was a ferment of newly discovered political and religious ideas. There was the spine-tingling news of revolution in France. Burke was writing his great political pamphlets. In Coleridge's room— the center of endless wine parties and bull sessions—there was no need to have the latest political tract on hand; Coleridge had always read it and could repeat whole pages verbatim. William Frend, a fellow at Jesus College, was expelled from Cambridge for his liberal politics and Unitarian religious convictions. Coleridge declared himself a Unitarian.

His debts grew, and an attempt to win a second scholarship failed. Coleridge wrote his brother George that for the entire six weeks preceding the examination he was "almost constantly intoxicated." For several months he tried to convince himself that he could pay off his debts by writing a great new translation of Greek and Latin lyric poetry. He never got around to it. A second plan was scarcely more practical: to win the Irish lottery! He even wrote a poem about it, "To Fortune," that was published in a London newspaper.

Coleridge went to London for the drawing. The outcome plunged him back into despair and thoughts of suicide. At this point, who could have guessed what Coleridge did next? Under the name of Silas Tomkyn Comberbacke (the initials corresponded to his own) he enlisted in the 15th Light Dragoons, a cavalry unit of the King's Regiment. Two days later he was sworn in—"an uncritical acceptance," writes Lawrence Hanson in his biography of Coleridge, "which the exigencies of war with France alone can explain."

Samuel Taylor Coleridge

"As a soldier of any kind," continues Hanson, "Coleridge would have been misplaced. As a cavalry man, he was a joke. He did not like horses: he could not ride: he was constantly thrown: he never learned to groom his horse: his accoutrements were never clean: he was constantly unwell."

Silas Tomkyn soon found himself cleaning the stables and serving as a hospital orderly. One day an officer, Captain Ogle, was startled to find the following epigraph scrawled on the white-washed stable wall: *Eheu! quam infortunii miserrimum est fuisse felicem!*

Coleridge's family obtained his discharge by providing a substitute, and in 1794 he was back at Jesus College, bubbling over with frugality and new resolutions. Two months later he was off with a friend on a walking tour of Wales. They stopped first at Oxford where Coleridge met Robert Southey, the second of his notable friendships. It was there that Coleridge, Southey, and some other young liberals—filled with enthusiasm for the French Revolution and with resentment against England—hatched up a utopian scheme that had even less chance of success than winning the Irish lottery.

The scheme was for twelve "gentlemen of good education and liberal principles" to get together with twelve like-minded ladies, leave England the following April, and establish a colony in North America, on the banks of the Susquehanna. This river valley was believed in England to be a spot of idyllic beauty; besides, Coleridge liked the sound of the river's name. All property was to be jointly owned. No money would be used. The men would work two or three hours a day. The women would keep house. A large library would be established. Everybody would be good, unselfish, and devoted to the commonweal and the cultivation of their minds. Coleridge called it Pantisocracy, combining the Greek words "panto" (all) and "isocracy": government by all, in contrast to England's hated aristocracy.

The young rebels took it all with incredible seriousness. Coleridge and his friend continued their tour of Wales, seeking money and converts. But, there was still the problem of Coleridge's helpmeet. He fancied himself still in love, "almost to madness," with a girl named Mary Evans, but

11

Mary had never taken him seriously as a prospective husband. Southey was engaged to Edith Fricker, who had a plump, pretty sister named Sarah. Soon everybody took it for granted that, come next spring, it would be Sarah who would accompany Coleridge to the Susquehanna. Coleridge forgot about Mary and for a time convinced himself that Sarah was his new love. "America! Southey! Miss Fricker!" he wrote to Southey. ". . . I certainly love her. I think of her incessantly . . ."

Mary caught wind of the scheme and wrote Coleridge a sensible but curious letter. "There is an eagerness in your nature which is ever hurrying you in the sad extreme. I have heard that you mean to leave England on a plan so absurd and extravagant that were I for a moment to imagine it *true*, I should be obliged . . . [to think you mad]." Although Mary closed by expressing sisterly affection for him, the letter subtly (perhaps with unconscious cruelty) aroused Coleridge's hopes of winning her after all, and he sent her a declaration of love. But soon she was engaged to marry somebody else. After writing a poem "On a Discovery Made too Late," Coleridge decided, reluctantly, that it was his duty to marry Sarah. A few weeks after Coleridge's wedding, Southey secretly married Edith and, on the same day, set sail alone for Portugal.

Though the gradual disintegration of Pantisocracy must have been painful to those concerned, it is impossible to read their letters today with a straight face. For one thing, Southey wanted to take along his aunt's faithful servant, Shadrach. When Coleridge found out that Southey intended Shad (as he was called) to remain a servant, he was furious. "To be employed in the toil of the field, while *we* are pursuing philosophical studies—can earldoms or emperorships boast so huge an inequality? . . . a *willing* slave is the worst of slaves! His *soul* is a slave." In addition, Southey also wanted to bring along some married couples and their children. But what if the children had already learned selfishness from their schoolfellows? "How are we to prevent their minds from infecting *our* children?" Coleridge wanted to know.

And so it went. The great plans dribbled off into nothing. Almost the only concrete results were a few mediocre sonnets that Coleridge wrote about Pantisocracy, and the following lines from his preposterous poem "To a Young Ass: Its Mother Being Tethered Near It":

> I hail thee *Brother*—spite of the fool's scorn!
> And fain would take thee with me, in the Dell
> Where high-soul'd Pantisocracy shall dwell!
> Where Mirth shall tickle Plenty's ribless side,
> And smiles from Beauty's Lip on sunbeams glide,
> Where Toil shall wed young Health that charming Lass!
> And use his sleek cows for a looking-glass—
> Where Rats shall mess with Terriers hand-in-glove
> And Mice with Pussy's Whiskers sport in Love.**2**

The first years of Coleridge's marriage were happy enough. He never returned to Cambridge for his degree. He and Sarah lived mostly on money borrowed from friends, and small sums that Coleridge obtained from sales of poetry. A periodical that he founded, *The Watchman* (published every eighth day to avoid a tax on weeklies), folded after the tenth issue. Coleridge admitted he probably lost 500 subscribers at one blow when he opened an essay "On National Fasts" by quoting Isaiah 16:11, "Wherefore my bowels shall sound like an harp . . ." He thought of becoming a Unitarian clergyman, and he tried unsuccessfully to open a school for children. Increasing rheumatic pains led to increasing use of opium. At Cambridge, during an attack of rheumatic fever

2. It was this poem, and others almost as bad, that Byron had in mind when he wrote (in *English Bards and Scotch Reviewers*, lines 255-64):

> Shall gentle Coleridge pass unnoticed here,
> To turgid ode and tumid stanza dear?
> Though themes of innocence amuse him best,
> Yet still Obscurity's a welcome guest.
> If Inspiration should her aid refuse
> To him who takes a Pixy for a muse,
> Yet none in lofty numbers can surpass
> The bard who soars to elegize an ass.
> So well his subject suits his noble mind,
> He brays, the Laureate of the long-eared kind.

and jaundice, the doctors had given him small doses of opium, and almost without realizing it he had slowly developed an addiction to the drug.

The year 1797 found the Coleridges living in the house of a friend at Stowey, in the southwestern county of Somerset. One morning Coleridge walked to Racedown, a nearby farm in Dorset, to renew a brief acquaintance with William Wordsworth and his small, shy, bright-eyed sister Dorothy who kept house for him. "He is a wonderful man . . ." was the way Dorothy described Coleridge in a letter to a friend. "At first I thought him very plain, that is, for about three minutes: he is pale and thin, has a wide mouth, thick lips, and not very good teeth, longish loose-growing half-curling rough black hair. But if you hear him speak for five minutes you think no more of them. His eye is large and full, not dark but grey;[3] such an eye as would receive from a heavy soul the dullest expression; but it speaks every emotion of his animated mind; it has more of the 'poet's eye in a fine frenzy rolling' than I ever witnessed. He has fine dark eyebrows, and an overhanging forehead."

It is interesting to compare Dorothy's famous description with the way Coleridge had pictured himself in a letter written six months earlier. "As to me, my face, unless animated by immediate eloquence, expresses great sloth, and great, indeed almost idiotic, good nature. 'Tis a mere carcase of a face: fat, flabby, and expressive chiefly of inexpression. Yet I am told that my eyes, eyebrows, and forehead are physiog-

3. There seems little doubt that Coleridge's eyes were grey; yet Carlyle spoke of them once as hazel and on another occasion as brown, Emerson (who as a young man paid Coleridge a visit) called them blue, and other descriptions of Coleridge record his eyes as greenish-gray and black. See "The Color of Coleridge's Eyes," by John Louis Haney, *Anglia*, Vol. 23, 1901, pp. 424-26.

nomically good; but of this the Deponent knoweth not. As to my shape, 'tis a good shape enough, if measured—but my gait is awkward, and the walk of the whole man indicates *indolence capable of energies* . . . I cannot breathe through my nose, so my mouth with sensual thick lips is almost always open."

Coleridge and Wordsworth were a study in contrast. Coleridge: outgoing, impulsive, emotional, unstable, weak-willed, impractical, helpless, careless; at times a liar and a hypocrite, but always fun-loving and lovable. (I refrain from adding that he was lazy, a frequent charge and one which he himself would advance. Coleridge was anything but lazy; he was this only in the sense that his wife would consider him lazy when he was reading, thinking, talking or writing instead of earning money, chopping wood, or taking out the garbage.) Wordsworth: cool, rational, industrious physically as well as intellectually, cautious, reserved, grim. Coleridge was as compulsive a talker as he was a reader. (Lamb once imagined himself button-holed by Coleridge and forced to escape by snipping off the button. Five hours later he returns, finds Coleridge, eyes closed, still holding the button and talking eloquently.) Surely Wordsworth must have been a compulsive listener. Yet the two men had much in common: a Protestant outlook, a love of nature, a love of poetry, enormous talent, and, it must also be said, a common conviction that Wordsworth was potentially the greatest poet in England.

Dorothy's role in this remarkable, mutually reinforcing triangle, has long been a favorite topic for critics and amateur Freudians. In spite of (or because of?) her intense, neurotic devotion to her brother, she and Coleridge became enormously fond of one another. They took long walks together through the rambling Quantock Hills. Many arresting phrases in Coleridge's poetry of this period, including some in *The Ancient Mariner,* are similar to phrases Dorothy used in a journal she was keeping. It has been difficult for scholars to determine who thought of what first. (Many of her phrases and suggestions *were* adopted, we know, by Wordsworth.)

There is no question of anything improper in their relationship, although below the surface, the emotional involvements of all three were doubtless subtle and complex. Here we need only note that the two men seemed desperately to need each other. Wordsworth, in Book X of the 1805 version of his *Prelude,* recalled a period of mental depression that had preceded the beginning of his friendship with Coleridge:

> Sick, wearied out with contrarieties,
> Yielded up moral questions in despair,
> And for my future studies, as the sole
> Employment of the enquiring faculty,
> Turn'd towards mathematics and their clear
> And solid evidence—Ah! then it was
> That Thou, most precious Friend! about this time
> First known to me, didst lend a living help
> To regulate my Soul. . . .

Both men profited hugely from the early years of their friendship, and through it all, Dorothy played her strange role as the indispensable catalyst. "Three people, but only one soul," was how Coleridge described it.

In July, 1797, the Wordsworths moved to Alfoxden, an old mansion that was but a short walk from Stowey. Their express purpose was to be closer to the Coleridges. For Coleridge, the next twelve months were pure joy. With one incredible leap he became a major poet. Almost all his finest poems—including that immortal fantasy trio, *The Ancient Mariner,* the first part of *Christabel,* and the fragment *Kubla Khan*—were written before the middle of the following year.

The genesis of *The Ancient Mariner* deserves detailed description. John Cruikshank, a neighbor, mentioned to Coleridge one day that he had had a strange dream about "a skeleton ship, with figures in it." This, together with some suggestions by Wordsworth, aroused in Coleridge a desire to write a sea ballad. The story was outlined by Coleridge on a long walk through the Quantock Hills that he, Wordsworth, and Dorothy made on November 13. This is how Wordsworth, years later, remembered the historic outing:

Samuel Taylor Coleridge

In the autumn of 1797, he [Coleridge], my sister, and myself started from Alfoxden pretty late in the afternoon with a view to visit Linton and the Valley of Stones near to it; and as our united funds were very small, we agreed to defray the expense of the tour by writing a poem to be sent to the *New Monthly Magazine*. Accordingly, we set off, and proceeded along the Quantock Hills towards Watchet; and in the course of this walk was planned the poem of the "Ancient Mariner," founded on a dream, as Mr. Coleridge said, of his friend Mr. Cruikshank. Much the greatest part of the story was Mr. Coleridge's invention, but certain parts I suggested; for example, some crime was to be committed which should bring upon the Old Navigator, as Coleridge afterwards delighted to call him, the spectral persecution, as a consequence of that crime and his own wanderings. I had been reading in Shelvocke's "Voyages," a day or two before, that while doubling Cape Horn, they frequently saw albatrosses in that latitude, the largest sort of sea fowl, some extending their wings twelve or thirteen feet. "Suppose," said I, "you represent him as having killed one of these birds on entering the South Sea, and that the tutelary spirits of these regions take upon them to avenge the crime." The incident was thought fit for the purpose, and adopted accordingly. I also suggested the navigation of the ship by the dead men, but do not recollect that I had anything more to do with the scheme of the poem. The gloss with which it was subsequently accompanied was not thought of by either of us at the time, at least, not a hint of it was given to me, and I have no doubt it was a gratuitous afterthought. We began the composition together on that, to me, memorable evening. I furnished two or three lines at the beginning of the poem, in particular

"And listened like a three years' child:
    The Mariner had his will."

These trifling contributions, all but one, which Mr. C has with unnecessary scrupulosity recorded, slipped out of his mind, as they well might. As we endeavored to proceed conjointly (I speak of the same evening), our respective manners proved so widely different that it would have been quite presumptuous in me to do anything but separate from an undertaking upon which I could only have been a clog. . . . The "Ancient Mariner" grew and grew till it became too important for our first object, which was limited to our expectations of five pounds; and we began to think of a volume which was to consist, as Mr. Coleridge has told the world, of poems chiefly on supernatural subjects, taken from common life, but looked at, as much as might be, through an imaginative medium.

Coleridge worked on the ballad for four months before he read it to Wordsworth and Dorothy on March 23, 1798. Compared to his early, conventional lyrics, even to his later poems, the ballad was something of a miracle. It seemed to spring out of Coleridge's skull with a fantastic life of its own. It was not at all the sort of poem one would have expected him to write. What does the old mariner's tale have to do, one is tempted to ask, with that young Greek scholar, compulsive talker, and moon-faced opium eater?

Yet somehow Coleridge did write it. For years he had been soaking up details from books on sea travel, perhaps in anticipation of a voyage to North America. His religious views were swinging from Unitarianism back to the orthodoxy of his parents. The opium that he took may have given a certain vividness and color to his reveries. He was 25, he had a good wife and a handsome year-old son, and one of England's greatest poets had become his friend. The times were ripe for the beginning of the Romantic movement with its emphasis on the wildness of nature, the charm of the distant past and distant places, its unconcealed emotion, its freedom to experiment with new poetic forms. And there was Dorothy's intelligent, sensitive enthusiasm. All these forces came together to produce the miracle.

It was, of course, Coleridge's greatest poem. No fantasy poem in English approaches its magic blend of beauty and terror. We know that he wrote it partly to defray the expenses of a trip. Could it have been that he wrote with a kind of youthful carelessness, and this very carelessness permitted a full, uninhibited release of creative imagination? It is as foolish to speak of *The Ancient Mariner* as "perfect" as it is to speak of one of Shakespeare's plays as perfect. Surely part of its magic lies in its roughness, ambiguity, and loose ends. Coleridge was always tinkering with it, altering lines, adding and removing stanzas, never quite sure of exactly what he was up to.

The ballad's first version appeared in a small book called *Lyrical Ballads,* 500 copies of which were published anonymously in September, 1798. Of the book's twenty-three poems, only four were by Coleridge. Nothing in the book indicated that more than one author was involved. Years later, this is how Coleridge remembered the way the book had been planned:

> During the first year that Mr. Wordsworth and I were neighbours, our conversations turned frequently on the two cardinal points of poetry, the power of exciting the sympathy of the reader by a faithful adherence to the truth of nature, and the power of giving the interest of novelty by the modifying colors of imagination. The sudden charm, which accidents of light and shade, which moon-light or sun-set, diffused over a known and familiar landscape, appeared to represent the practicability of combining both. These are the poetry of nature. The thought suggested itself (to which of us I do not recollect) that a series of poems might be composed of two sorts. In the one, the incidents and agents were to be, in part at least, supernatural; and the excellence aimed at was to consist in the interesting of the affections by the dramatic truth of such emotions, as would naturally accompany such situations, supposing them real. And real in *this* sense they have been to every human being who, from whatever source of delusion, has at any time believed himself under supernatural agency. For the second class, subjects were to be chosen from ordinary life; the characters and incidents were to be such, as will be found in every village and its vicinity, where there is a meditative and feeling mind to seek after them, or to notice them, when they present themselves.
>
> In this idea originated the plan of the *Lyrical Ballads;* in which it was agreed, that my endeavours should be directed to persons and characters supernatural, or at least romantic; yet so as to transfer from our inward

nature a human interest and a semblance of truth sufficient to procure for these shadows of imagination that willing suspension of disbelief for the moment, which constitutes poetic faith. Mr. Wordsworth, on the other hand, was to propose to himself as his object, to give the charm of novelty to things of every day, and to excite a feeling analogous to the supernatural, by awakening the mind's attention from the lethargy of custom, and directing it to the loveliness and the wonders of the world before us; an inexhaustible treasure, but for which, in consequence of the film of familiarity and selfish solicitude we have eyes, yet see not, ears that hear not, and hearts that neither feel nor understand.

Things did not work out as planned. Only *The Ancient Mariner* actually fulfilled Coleridge's intention.4 "I wrote *The Ancient Mariner,* and was preparing among other poems, *The Dark Ladie,* and the *Christabel,* in which I should have more nearly realized my ideal, than I had done in my first attempt. But Mr. Wordsworth's industry had proved so much more successful, and the number of his poems so much greater, that my compositions, instead of forming a balance, appeared rather an interpolation of heterogeneous matter."

Although *Lyrical Ballads* eventually became one of the

---

4. Intended for *Lyrical Ballads,* though not included, was Wordsworth's narrative poem "Peter Bell," in which he sought to dramatize the same moral theme of Coleridge's ballad, but without resort to the supernatural. Parallels with *The Ancient Mariner* are so obvious, and the poetry so inept, that the poem is almost a parody. Peter Bell, a wanderer by land instead of sea, is an uncouth, immoral salesman of (Wedgwood?) pottery, blind to the beauty of yellow primroses and other aspects of nature:

Not for the moon cared he a tittle
And for the stars he cared as little.

An act of cruelty to one of God's humble creatures, a donkey, plunges him into a sequence of terrifying events which lead finally to his remorse, repentance, and spiritual rebirth. There are numerous, deliberate attempts to introduce images from Coleridge's ballad: a man's corpse, a horned moon, moonlight, blood, the donkey's shining eye, a grotesque grin, auroral lights, an apparition, those three mystic numbers (3, 7, and 9), the great harlot of Babylon, an empty bucket, an underground explosion, and many others.

great milestones in English poetry, heralding the beginning of the Romantic movement, its sales were poor and its critical reception no better. Coleridge later recalled (in *Table Talk*) that he had been told by the publisher that most of the book's sales had been to sailors who, having heard of *The Ancient Mariner,* thought it was a naval songbook. "The *Lyrical Ballads* are not liked at all by any," was the way Mrs. Coleridge bluntly put it in a letter. Nobody appreciated Wordsworth's fine poem, "Lines Written a Few Miles above Tintern Abbey," which closed the book. No reviewer perceived the greatness of *The Ancient Mariner* which opened it. Most critics complained that they couldn't understand the ballad. "The extravagance of a mad German poet," said one. "The strangest story of a cock and a bull that we ever saw on paper . . . a rhapsody of unintelligible wildness and incoherence," said another.

Coleridge was deeply wounded by Southey's review, particularly because he knew that Southey knew him to be the ballad's author:

> In a very different style of poetry is the *Rime of the Ancient Mariner;* a ballad (says the advertisement) "professedly written in imitation of the *style,* as well as the spirit of the elder poets." We are tolerably conversant with the early English poets; and can discover no resemblance whatever, except in antiquated spelling and a few obsolete words. This piece appears to us perfectly original in style as well as in story. Many of the stanzas are laboriously beautiful; but in connection they are absurd or unintelligible. Our readers may exercise their ingenuity in attempting to unriddle what follows:
>
> > "The roaring wind, it roar'd far off.
> > It did not come anear." etc., etc.
>
> We do not sufficiently understand the story to analyse it. It is a Dutch attempt at German sublimity. Genius has here been employed in producing a poem of little merit.

(I sometimes fancy that Southey's punishment is that his career as a poet would be almost forgotten today were it not for Lewis Carroll's "You are Old Father William," which parodies one of his poems. It is hard to believe that Southey, like Wordsworth, was once poet laureate of England and that his collected verse fills ten volumes.)

Coleridge himself, who always enjoyed literary jokes, joined in the general criticism of his ballad. In *Biographia Literaria* he recalls:

The following anecdote will not be wholly out of place here, and may perhaps amuse the reader. An amateur performer in verse expressed to a common friend a strong desire to be introduced to me, but hesitated in accepting my friend's immediate offer, on the score that "he was, he must acknowledge, the author of a confounded severe epigram on my *Ancient Mariner,* which had given me great pain." I assured my friend that, if the epigram was a good one, it would only increase my desire to become acquainted with the author, and begged to hear it recited: when, to my no less surprise than amusement, it proved to be one which I had myself some time before written and inserted in the "Morning Post," to wit—

To the Author of the Ancient Mariner.
Your poem must eternal be,
Dear sir! it cannot fail,
For 'tis incomprehensible,
And without head or tail.

Neither Coleridge nor Wordsworth was in England at the time *Lyrical Ballads* and its first reviews appeared. Together with Dorothy they had gone to Germany. Coleridge had recently received an annuity from his friends the Wedgwood brothers (sons of Josiah Wedgwood, the famous potter) with the proviso that he *not* become a minister, but devote all his energies to literature and philosophy. (The German trip was a bonus; the Wedgwoods footed the bill for all three travelers!) Coleridge had been studying German and was anxious to make firsthand contact with German philosophy. It was while in Germany that he learned of the death of his second child, Berkeley, born shortly before he left. Coleridge's letters to Sarah are filled with genuine concern for her and tender sorrow over the loss of his child. But he did not return.

Samuel Taylor Coleridge

After eleven months abroad, Coleridge finally meandered home. His relations with Sarah deteriorated rapidly. Wordsworth, having at last recovered from a careless romance in France with Annette Vallon, the girl who bore his illegitimate daughter, became engaged to his cousin Mary Hutchinson. And now a nightmarish parody of the past unfolded.

You will recall that Sarah, Coleridge's wife, had been the sister of Southey's fiancée. Wordsworth's fiancée also had a sister named Sarah, with whom Coleridge proceeded to fall violently in love. The precise nature of their relationship is still a puzzle for historians; none of her letters to Coleridge survive, and only a few of his to her, so there is little to go on except speculation. She was a small, plump, brown-haired girl, two years younger than Coleridge, not pretty, but with a fair skin and, above all, a lively sense of humor. So far as anyone knows, their relationship was as non-physical as it was hopeless (divorce in those days was almost unthinkable); nevertheless, there is no doubt about the passion with which Coleridge was smitten. A notebook contains an entry in Latin in which he speaks of pressing her hand one Sunday, standing around the fire after an occasion of "Conundrums and Puns and Stories and Laughter," and how love had then pierced him like an arrow, "poisoned, alas, and incurable." A later entry recalls her "dear lips" pressed to his forehead. The obsession lasted ten years, and was certainly one of the causes of the eventual decline of friendship between Coleridge and Wordsworth. Sarah Hutchinson never married. She finally moved in with the Wordsworths and Dorothy to become a sort of third wife.

Coleridge's poem "Love" (later so widely imitated—it was the prototype of Keats's "La Belle Dame sans Merci") was a disguised expression of his first outburst of love for Sarah Hutchinson. "Dejection: an Ode," composed two years later, expresses the utter hopelessness of his emotions:

> A grief without a pang, void, dark, and drear,
>   A stifled, drowsy, unimpassioned grief,
> Which finds no natural outlet, no relief,
>   In word, or sigh, or tear—

There is a sad entry in Dorothy's journal: "William and

I sauntered in the garden. Coleridge came to us, and repeated the verses he wrote to Sara. I was affected with them, and . . . in miserable spirits. The sunshine, the green fields, and the fair sky made me sadder; even the little happy sporting lambs seemed but sorrowful to me . . . I went to bed after dinner, could not sleep."

The two Sarahs have, understandably, often been confused by Coleridge's biographers. In his letters and notebooks, Coleridge always dropped the "h" from both names, and to make matters more confusing, in 1802 he named his daughter Sara. Sometimes, to distinguish the first from the second Sarah, he rearranged the letters of "Sara" (Hutchinson) to spell "Asra." Some forty love poems, now called the Asra poems, are known to have been written to the second Sarah. (The interested reader should consult Thomas M. Raysor's "Coleridge and 'Asra,' " *Studies in Philology*, July, 1929, and George Whalley's book, *Coleridge and Sara Hutchinson and the Asra Poems,* 1955.)

When a new edition of *Lyrical Ballads* came out in 1800 under Wordsworth's name, Coleridge's contribution to the book remained anonymous. *The Ancient Mariner* came close to being left out. "From what I can gather," Wordsworth had earlier written to the publisher, "it seems that The Ancyent Marinere has upon the whole been an injury to the volume, I mean that the old words and the strangeness of it have deterred readers from going on . . . If the volume should come to a second edition I would put in its place some little things which would be more likely to suit the public taste."

But the poem remained. Coleridge had revised it considerably, taking out many of the more obscure old English expressions about which critics had complained, and adding to it the subtitle: "A Poet's Reverie." Wordsworth's note, added to the new edition, comments patronizingly:

I cannot refuse myself the gratification of informing such Readers as may have been pleased with this Poem, or with any part of it, that they owe their pleasure in some sort to me; as the Author was himself very desirous that it should be suppressed. This wish had arisen from a consciousness of the defects of the Poem, and from a knowledge that many persons had been much displeased with it. The Poem of my Friend has indeed great defects; first, that the principal person has no distinct character, either in his profession of Mariner, or as a human being who having been long under the control of supernatural impressions might be supposed himeslf to partake of something supernatural: secondly, that he does not act, but is continually acted upon: thirdly, that the events having no necessary connection do not produce each other; and lastly, that the imagery is somewhat too laboriously accumulated. Yet the Poem contains many delicate touches of passion, and indeed the passion is everywhere true to nature; a great number of the stanzas present beautiful images, and are expressed with unusual felicity of language; and the versification, though the metre is itself unfit for long poems, is harmonious and artfully varied, exhibiting the utmost powers of that metre, and every variety of which it is capable. It therefore appeared to me that these several merits (the first of which, namely that of the passion, is of the highest kind), gave to the Poem a value which is not often possessed by better Poems. On this account I requested of my Friend to permit me to republish it.

Charles Lamb, quick to defend the poem earlier against Southey's attack, was equally miffed by the way it had been treated and commented upon in the new edition. He wrote to Wordsworth:

> I am sorry that Coleridge has christened his *Ancient Marinere,* a *Poet's Reverie;* it is as bad as Bottom the Weaver's declaration that he is not a lion, but only the scenical representation of a lion. What new idea is gained by this title but one subversive of all credit— which the tale should force upon us—of its truth.**5**

5. It is hard to believe, but one of the most persistent approaches to *The Ancient Mariner* is to regard it as not about the supernatural at all. William Darby Templeman, summarizing the poem for *Encyclopedia Americana,* says: "Though often regarded as a poem of the supernatural, *The Ancient Mariner* is rather one of abnormal psychology, in which a poor workman, illiterate, profoundly superstitious, and at least partly crazed by long exposure, fear, and loneliness, is presented as giving his own account of the happenings . . ."

More recently, Lionel Stevenson, in *"The Ancient Mariner* as a Dramatic Monolog" (*The Personalist,* January, 1949), interprets the ballad as a dramatic story about a superstitious sailor who imagines that killing a bird has caused all his woes. The moral quatrain at the end is, says Stevenson, not Coleridge's idea of a moral, but only his idea of the Mariner's idea of a moral: "the stumbling effort of a man with no rudiment of intellectual training to formulate his sense of religious dedication to universal love and brotherhood . . ."

For me, I was never so affected with any human tale. After first reading it, I was totally possessed with it for many days. I dislike all the miraculous part of it; but the feelings of the man under the operation of such scenery, dragged me along like Tom Piper's magic whistle. I totally differ from your idea that the Marinere should have had a character and profession. This is a beauty in *Gulliver's Travels,* where the mind is kept in a placid state of little wonderments; but the Ancient Marinere undergoes such trials as overwhelm and bury all individuality or memory of what he was—like the state of a man in a bad dream, one terrible peculiarity of which is, that all consciousness of personality is gone. Your other observation is, I think as well, a little unfounded: the Marinere, from being conversant in supernatural events, *has* acquired a supernatural and strange cast of phrase, eye, appearance, etc., which frighten the wedding guest. You will excuse my remarks, because I am hurt and vexed that you should think it necessary, with a prose apology, to open the eyes of dead men that cannot see.

To sum up a general opinion of the second volume, I do not feel any one poem in it so forcibly as the *Ancient Marinere,* and the *Mad Mother,* and the *Lines at Tintern Abbey,* in the first.

In 1800 a third son, Derwent, was born to Coleridge and Sarah, and two years later, the daughter they named Sara. But their marriage was beyond repair and by 1806 the break was complete. They separated informally. From that time on, Sarah and the two children were cared for by Southey, with the help of friends. Later, Coleridge transferred his annuity to his wife; from time to time he was able to send her small sums from the sales of his prose works.

For fifteen years after his return from Germany, Coleridge wandered here and there, sponging off friends. He would pop in for a short visit, and stay months. Wordsworth, Byron, and De Quincey were among the notables who came to his rescue with considerable loans. For a short time he was Secretary to the Governor of Malta. He visited Rome. He tried to edit a new magazine called *The Friend,* but it was as badly managed as *The Watchman* and soon failed. In 1809 he rejoined Wordsworth in the Lake District, where Wordsworth and his three women had settled, but their friendship had cooled and their ways soon separated again. His play *Remorse* had a short, successful run at Drury Lane Theatre, in London, thanks largely to Byron's help and influence.

It was in Germany that Kant took hold of Coleridge, "as with a giant's hand"—an event which, as Bertrand Russell has observed in his *History of Western Philosophy,* "did not improve his verse." Indeed, Coleridge never did recapture the magic of that wonderful year at Stowey; his energies turned more and more toward the study of German philosophy and theology. As a kind of literary character, like Samuel Johnson before him, his fame spread around the world. He was much in demand as a lecturer: on Shakespeare, Milton, poetry, drama, philosophy, and religion. Coleridge was a brilliant conversationalist (or rather, monologist, for he seldom listened to what anyone else said), but unimpressive on the platform. On many occasions he even failed to appear. When he did, his lectures had a feeble, absent-minded quality. They rambled off on everything except the main topic. Nobody understood him when he tried to explain German idealism. Byron wrote, in his Dedication to *Don Juan:*

> And Coleridge, too, has lately taken wing,
> But like a hawk encumber'd with his hood,—
> Explaining metaphysics to the nation—
> I wish he would explain his explanation.

Coleridge so constantly altered his philosophic and religious views that it is hard to pin down exactly what he believed, at any given time, about a variety of important topics. Yet there is one dominating thread of intent that ties together the history of his shifting metaphysical opinions. Throughout his adult life he was searching desperately for a firm philosophical underpinning to support his Protestant faith. He believed that the Catholic philosophers had perverted reason by trying to prove too much, and that only along the lines indicated by Kant, who destroyed reason to make room for faith, could one finally reconcile the head of modern science with the heart of Christianity.

At no time, except for a brief period as a youth when he was reading Voltaire, did Coleridge cease to be a true believer; not even during his Unitarian period. Most Unitarians today are agnostics or atheists, but in Coleridge's day they were Christian theists who stressed the humanity of Jesus in opposition to trinitarianism. After his return from Germany, Coleridge abandoned Unitarianism completely. Take away the divinity of Christ, he wrote, and God becomes no more than a "power in darkness," like the power of gravitation. A letter written in 1802 to his brother George contains the following capsule version of his faith:

"My faith is simply this—that there is an original corruption in our nature, from which and from the consequences of which, we may be redeemed by Christ—not, as the Socinians [Catholic heretics, forerunners of the Unitarians] say, by his pure morals, or excellent example merely—but in a mysterious manner as an effect of his Crucifixion. And this I believe, not because I *understand* it; but because I *feel* that it is not only suitable to, but needful for my nature, and because I find it clearly revealed. Whatever the New Testament says I believe—according to my best judgment of the meaning of the sacred writer."

Though Coleridge sometimes expressed one set of views to his brother George while professing other views to his friends, there is no reason to doubt the sincerity of the passage just quoted. It is easy to forget that Coleridge, like Milton, was one of those rare birds in English literature, a genuine Protestant poet. Many lines of his poems, including some in *The Ancient Mariner*, reflect his doctrinal beliefs.

He may have been inconsistent at times, unsure of many things, weak in behavior, but only confusion results when a critic tries to sweep Coleridge's Protestant convictions under the rug, as though they were somehow irrelevant to his life and writings.

"Every man is born," Coleridge said (*Table Talk*, July 2, 1830), "an Aristotelian or a Platonist." The distinction can be made in many different ways. Let's say a Platonist is one who believes (as an Aristotelian does not) that this world is only a shadow of a larger reality; a reality utterly beyond the comprehension of our little animal minds. ". . . and we in this low world / Placed with our backs to bright Reality," was how Coleridge put it in *Destiny of Nations.* In this sense he was a born Platonist. As a young man he was fascinated for a time by Neoplatonism and the even wilder pantheistic occultism of Jacob Boehme, but his first really great philosophical enthusiasm was for the gentle, common-sense, almost colorless Platonism of David Hartley.

Hartley was a medical doctor of unorthodox Protestant views, famous in his day for a two-volume work, *Observations on Man, his Frame, Duty, and Expectations.* The work was an ambitious attempt to harmonize the empiricism of science, and the views of such empirical philosophers as David Hume, with what Hartley considered the essentials of Christianity. Though few people read Hartley today, the first half of his work says little with which a modern empiricist would disagree. Hartley's doctrine of the "association of ideas" as the basis of animal habit and thought is now generally accepted. His "vibrations" in the ether, by means of which sensory experience is carried along nerves and stored in the brain, are clearly equivalent to today's "electrical impulses" that transmit ingeniously coded information along the nerve fibers. Finally, Hartley was a thoroughgoing determinist, or "necessitarian," as such philosophers were called then. Allowing for his lack of knowledge of twentieth century science, his views are almost indistinguishable from those of most modern psychologists.

The second half of Hartley's opus is another matter. The

entire empirical outlook of the first volume is now framed
by Christian theology. *This* world, with its unvarying laws,
its vibrating ether, its creatures with the remarkable power
of storing and associating vibrations in their heads—*this* is
the world that God made. Tens of thousands of liberal
Protestant ministers today hold opinions differing in no
essential respect from Hartley's "system." For Coleridge, the
book was a liberation. He named his first child David
Hartley. There is no question that many of Hartley's tenets
underlie portions of *The Ancient Mariner,* especially
Hartley's insistence that animals share with man the power
of associative thought, and that they possess low-order souls
and are therefore united with man as part of one unified
divine creation.[6]

But by the time his second child was born, Coleridge was
beginning to have doubts about Hartley's "Christian mate-
rialism," as it was sometimes called. He was particularly
disturbed by its dogmatic denial of free will. "Berkeley," the
name given to his second son, reflects Coleridge's enthusiasm
for the idealistic system of another Protestant philosopher,
Bishop Berkeley. This interest, in turn, was supplanted by
his discovery of Kant, and his growing preoccupation with
those German idealists who were Kant's successors.

Kant was, of course, still another philosopher in the
Protestant tradition. His special brand of idealism had a

[6] The influence of Hartley's views
in general on the poem has been
emphasized by Dorothy Waples in
"David Hartley in *The Ancient
Mariner"* (*Journal of English and
Germanic Philology,* July, 1936).
Solomon Francis Gingerich, in a
paper reprinted in *Essays in the
Romantic Poets,* 1924, stresses the
influence of Hartley's determinism
on the ballad; not determinism in
the modern scientific sense, but in
the Calvinistic sense of all events
in nature and history being fore-
ordained by God.

prodigious influence on German theology, and Coleridge struggled for years trying to master the involutions of post-Kantian metaphysics. He finally concluded that Kant's views had reached their purest form in the philosophy of Friedrich von Schelling. It was Coleridge's fervid hope that someday he would write a vast systematic work on metaphysics in which he would give the world his version of Platonism, expanded and refined by Christian orthodoxy and German idealism. ("Jesus Christ," he once declared, "was a Platonic philosopher.") Alas, it was only one of the many grandiose plans about which Coleridge talked and wrote at length, but never carried out. After his death, one of his disciples, Joseph Henry Green, produced a two-volume work entitled *Spiritual Philosophy: Founded on the Teaching of the Late S. T. Coleridge.* But neither this volume nor any of Coleridge's scattered metaphysical writings succeeded in explaining Coleridge's explanation, or making any significant contribution to idealistic philosophy or Protestant theology.

Nevertheless, Coleridge acquired an enormous reputation in his day as an interpreter of German thought. He was essentially a literary thinker, a stimulator, a prodder; he was not a systematic thinker. Yet his influence on Emerson and the New England transcendentalists was strong, and there is no question that he belongs in that tradition that leads up through Kierkegaard and on into the neoorthodoxy of twentieth-century Protestantism. Coleridge's *Letters on the Inspiration of the Scriptures,* for example, could almost have been written by Paul Elmer More, or C. S. Lewis, or Karl Barth. Even the "yea" and "nay" of the Barthian dialectic reverberate through Coleridge's third letter.

The older Coleridge became, the heavier he used opium. It was a habit he could not shake, and a never-ceasing source of misery, both physical and spiritual. His nightmares became more frequent, more severe. He felt himself approaching madness. One of his letters to Dr. James Gillman, a physician and friend, was a heart-rending plea for help in escaping from "the terror that haunts my mind." The final eighteen years of his sad, slovenly life were spent in Dr. Gillman's home, at Highgate, where his opium doses could be carefully kept to a minimum.

It was at Highgate that "Christabel" and "Kubla Khan" (the first started and the second completed back in his Stowey period) were first published. The thin volume also included his poem "Pains of Sleep," in which he speaks of waking up screaming from a "fiendish dream," weeping, wondering why such sufferings had come to him. The poem closes with those pathetic lines:

> To be beloved is all I need,
> And whom I love, I love, indeed.

In 1817 his collected poems appeared in a volume called *Sibylline Leaves*. It contained his final revision of *The Ancient Mariner*. The marginal gloss—such glosses were common in the sea travel books of the time—and the motto from Burnet were first added to this printing, although Coleridge may have written his gloss many years earlier. It was the first occasion on which the poem was publicly identified as his own. *Lay Sermons, Biographia Literaria,* and *Aids to Reflection* were among his prose books published while he was under Dr. Gillman's care. His last book, *Church and State,* appeared in 1830. (*Confessions of an Inquiring Spirit* and *Table Talk* were not issued until after his death.)

Thomas Carlyle visited Coleridge at Highgate. His vivid, unsympathetic description is often quoted, but is worth quoting again:

Coleridge sat on the brow of Highgate Hill in those years, looking down on London and its smoke tumult like a sage escaped from the inanity of life's battle, attracting towards him the thoughts of innumerable brave souls still engaged there. His express contributions to poetry, philosophy, or any specific province of human literature or enlightenment had been small and sadly intermittent; but he had, especially among young inquiring men, a higher than literary, a kind of prophetic or magician character. He was thought to hold—he alone in England—the key of German and other Transcendentalisms; knew the sublime secret of believing by the "reason" what the "understanding" had been obliged to fling out as incredible; and could still, after Hume and Voltaire had done their best and worst with him, profess himself an orthodox Christian, and say and print to the Church of England, with its singular old rubrics and surplices at Allhallowtide, *Esto perpetua*. A sublime man; who alone in those dark days had saved his crown of spiritual manhood, escaping from the black materialisms and revolutionary deluges with "God, Freedom, Immortality," still his; a king of men. The practical intellects of the world did not much heed him, or carelessly reckoned him a metaphysical dreamer; but to the rising spirits of the young generation he had this dusky sublime character, and sat there as a kind of Magus, girt in mystery and enigma; his Dodona oak-grove (Mr. Gillman's house at Highgate) whispering strange things, uncertain whether oracles or jargon.

* * * *

The good man—he was now getting old, towards sixty perhaps, and gave you the idea of a life that had been full of sufferings; a life heavy-laden, half-vanquished, still swimming painfully in seas of manifold physical and other bewilderment. Brow and head were round and of massive weight, but the face was flabby and irresolute. The deep eyes, of a light hazel, were as full of sorrow as of inspiration; confused pain looked mildly from them, as in a kind of mild astonishment. The whole figure and air, good and amiable otherwise, might be called flabby and irresolute; expressive of weakness under possibility of strength. He hung loosely on his limbs, with knees bent, and stooping attitude; in walking he rather shuffled than decisively stept; and a lady once remarked he never could fix which side of the gardenwalk would suit him best, but continually shifted, corkscrew fashion, and kept trying both; a heavy-laden, high-aspiring, and surely much-suffering man. His voice, naturally soft and good, had contracted itself into a plaintive snuffle and sing-song; he spoke as if preaching—you could have said preaching earnestly and almost hopelessly the weightiest things. I still recollect his "object" and "subject," terms of continual recurrence in the Kantean province; and how he sang and snuffled them into "om-m-ject" and "sum-m-mject," with a kind of solemn shake or quaver as he rolled along. No talk in his century or in any other could be more surprising.

Coleridge died in Dr. Gillman's house on July 25, 1834. His funeral was unattended by his wife, children, or three old friends. Southey reacted coolly to news of his friend's death. A shaken Wordsworth declared that Coleridge was the most "wonderful" man he had ever known. It was Charles Lamb, his first good friend, who was most grief stricken. "His great and dear spirit haunts me," Lamb wrote. "Never saw I his likeness, nor probably the world can see again."

PART II

The Rime of the Ancient Mariner

from Coleridge's *Poetical Works*, 1834

1. The passage has been translated as follows:

I readily believe that there are more invisible beings in the universe than visible. But who will declare to us the nature of all these, the rank, relationships, distinguishing characteristics and qualities of each? What is it they do? Where is it they dwell? Always the human intellect circles around the knowledge of these mysteries, never touching the centre. Meanwhile it is, I deny not, ofttimes well pleasing to behold sketched upon the mind, as upon a tablet, a picture of the greater and better world; so shall not the spirit, wonted to the petty concerns of daily life, narrow itself over-much, nor sink utterly into trivialities. But meanwhile we must diligently seek after truth, and maintain a temperate judgment, if we would distinguish certainty from uncertainty, day from night.

Thomas Burnet, an English theologian of the seventeenth century, is remembered today only because he wrote one of the funniest books in the history of Protestant pseudo-science: *Telluris Theoria Sacra (Sacred Theory of the Earth)*, London, 1681. Before the Flood, Burnet argues, the earth was hollow, filled with water, and perfectly smooth like an egg. There were no seas, no valleys, and no mountains. The climate was perpetually spring-like, the sunny weather broken only by occasional gentle rains. But men were long-lived, like Methuselah, which gave them plenty of leisure time for wickedness. God destroyed the corrupt earth by crushing it until the shell cracked, letting out the waters of the deluge. Once egg-perfect, the earth now became a "rude lump . . . a little dirty planet." The crumpled shell formed mountains. The flood waters collected in low areas to make the oceans. Burnet's opinion of the sea as "the most ghastly thing in nature," may have found its way into many of Coleridge's stanzas. Burnet also had an interesting theory about comets. He thought they were literally "flying hells," abodes for the damned.

Sacred Theory of the Earth aroused considerable controversy, but most Anglican divines welcomed it as a brilliant reconciliation of science and Scripture. Samuel Johnson thought highly of it. Addison praised it in a Latin ode, and Steele devoted an issue of *The Spectator* to it. (One thinks—and a sobering thought it is—of how Immanuel Velikovsky's equally preposterous and somewhat similar theories have been taken seriously in our day by *Harper's* magazine.) The reader must not suppose, however, that astronomy was so primitive in Burnet's time that a well-informed man was justified in holding such views. Quite the contrary. As late as 1722, when Burnet issued the sixth edition of his *Sacred Theory,* he was still battling Newton and defending the view that the earth was fixed, with the heavens revolving around it. Of course this doesn't mean that Burnet was not a cultured man who wrote well in Latin; it merely indicates that he was a one-culture man, profoundly ignorant of the science of his day.

Like so many literary figures of his time (and ours!), Coleridge had only a superficial understanding of science and a tendency to take seriously most of the pseudo-scientific cults with which he came in con-

The Rime of the Ancient Mariner

IN SEVEN PARTS

Facile credo, plures esse Naturas invisibiles quam visibiles in rerum universitate. Sed horum omnium familiam quis nobis enarrabit? et gradus et cognationes et discrimina et singulorum munera? Quid agunt? quae loca habitant? Harum rerum notitiam semper ambivit ingenium humanum, nunquam attigit. Juvat, interea, non diffiteor, quandoque in animo, tanquam in tabulà, majoris et melioris mundi imaginem contemplari: ne mens assuefacta hodiernae vitae minutiis se contrahat nimis, et tota subsidat in pusillas cogitationes. Sed veritati interea invigilandum est, modusque servandus, ut certa ab incertis, diem a nocte, distinguamus.

—T. BURNET, *Archaeol. Phil.* p. 68.[1]

tact. In *Table Talk,* for example, we find him commenting favorably —though with reservations—on both homeopathy and phrenology. As a Protestant fundamentalist he was eager to harmonize science with Old Testament history, so it is not hard to understand why he would find Burnet's *Sacred Theory* so fascinating. Like Plato's *Dialogs* (he wrote in Chap. 14 of *Biographia Literaria*) the book provides "undeniable proofs that poetry of the highest kind may exist without metre . . ." He even considered, at one time, translating the entire volume into blank verse! (For ways in which the book undoubtedly influenced lines in *The Ancient Mariner*—especially the reference to a "bloody sun" in Part II, St. 7—see Lowes's *The Road to Xanadu,* Chap. X.)

The success of *Sacred Theory* won Burnet a position at court, but he shattered his own career by writing *Archaeologiae Philosophicae,* from which Coleridge took the quotation given at the top of his poem. In this book Burnet dared to suggest that the Biblical account of the Fall was allegory, not history. The king was obliged to discharge him.

The poem's epigraph is not an exact quotation from Burnet; there are a few changes and additions, and many lines from the middle of the quotation are left out. Some of the omitted lines may have influenced parts of the ballad's gloss. For a translation of the complete passage, see *The Notebooks of Samuel Taylor Coleridge,* edited by Kathleen Coburn, Vol. I, Part 2, Note 1000H.

PART I

2. The abrupt beginning is characteristic of many old English ballads. ("It was a knight in Scotland born," for example, is the opening line of "The Fair Flower of Northumberland.")

"The keynote of the whole poem is sounded in the words *Ancient Mariner*," writes Julian W. Abernathy, an early commentator, "suggesting the remote, strange, weird, and uncanny. The effect of the phrase throughout the poem is worth special study. Change the words anywhere to their verbal equivalent, *Old Sailor*, and note . . . the difference of meaning and effect."

3. In keeping with earlier ballads and tales of the supernatural, Coleridge's poem stresses the traditionally mystic numbers 3, 7, and 9. For other uses of 3, see lines 15, 198, 508. For 7, see lines 261, 552, and note that the ballad has seven Parts. For 9, see lines 76, 133, 377.

4. It is no accident that this first stanza is so similar in structure to the first stanza of what Coleridge (in his "Dejection: An Ode") calls "The grand old ballad of Sir Patrick Spence."

> The king sits in Dumferling toune,
>   Drinking the blude-reid wine:
> "O whar will I get guid sailor,
>   To sail this schip of mine?"

In his opening stanza, Coleridge establishes the basic, traditional stanza form of the old English ballad. As the poem proceeds, this form is modified in all sorts of subtle ways that prevent it from becoming dull and repetitive (see Note 18). The use of internal rhyme, for instance, puts in its first appearance in the third line of the next stanza.

5. The carefree merriment of the wedding feast—which frames the poem, so to speak, by its presence at both the beginning and the end —serves to intensify by contrast the desolation and horror of the Mariner's tale. In the ballad's first version, third stanza, the contrast is further emphasized by the Wedding-Guest's suggestion that if the Mariner has a "laughsome tale" to tell, he can come to the feast and amuse the guests. Laughsome tale, indeed!

Note how the Wedding-Guest's omission of "you," in the stanza's last line, suggests impatience to be on his way.

6. A clownish, awkward, ill-bred fellow. The slang expression "loony" (from lunatic) did not become current until late in the nineteenth century, though the association of this word with the Wedding-Guest's "loon" is not inappropriate.

7. Eftsoons: Immediately.

PART I

An ancient
Mariner meeteth
three Gallants
bidden to a
wedding-feast,
and detaineth
one.

It is an ancient Mariner,**2**
* And he stoppeth one of three.**3**
"By thy long grey beard and glittering
    eye,
Now wherefore stopp'st thou me?**4**

The Bridegroom's doors are opened wide,
And I am next of kin;
The guests are met, the feast is set:
May'st hear the merry din."**5**

He holds him with his skinny hand,
10   "There was a ship," quoth he.
"Hold off! unhand me, grey-beard loon!"**6**
Eftsoons his hand dropt he.**7**

* *Indicates line of poem illustrated*

39

8. Ocular "fascination," a miraculous power said to emanate from the eyes of certain individuals, is a superstition well nigh universal throughout the world from ancient times to the present. In extreme form, the power of the "evil eye" could blight crops, shatter mirrors, injure animals and men, even kill. Special laws concerning it were passed by the Romans. Thousands of charms, rituals, and amulets have been devised to counteract it, especially in India and the Far East. The possessor of an evil eye was not necessarily evil himself; the power was sometimes regarded as an unfortunate talent over which the possessor had no control. On the other hand, witches, wizards, and demons were often said to possess an evil eye, and limited powers of ocular fascination are common attributes of villains in countless older works of fiction and drama.

In Coleridge's day few enlightened people believed in the more extreme manifestations of the power; but almost everyone supposed that snakes possessed "glittering eyes" with which they paralyzed prey, and it was widely believed that hypnotists possessed similar ocular powers. Mesmerism was then enjoying a vogue in London. Coleridge probably attended demonstrations in which he saw the wills of persons and animals frozen by what appeared to be the occult power of a mesmerist's gaze. That Coleridge had such power in mind when he spoke of the Mariner's "glittering eye" is evident in Part V, Stanza 18 of the poem as it was first written:

> Listen, O listen, thou Wedding-guest!
> "Marinere! thou hast thy will:
> "For that, which comes out of thine eye, doth make
> "My body and soul to be still."

Geraldine, the witch in Coleridge's poem "Christabel," has the power of the evil eye. Although her eyes normally are large and beautiful, they shrink at times to the beady eyes of a snake. In his poem "The Nightingale," Coleridge speaks of how his infant son's eyes "did glitter in the yellow moon-beam," though here, of course, there is no suggestion of evil. (Note line 437, *The Ancient Mariner*, in which the stony eyes of the dead sailors glitter in the moonlight.) More than one commentator has said that Coleridge himself, in his power to hold listeners entranced by his conversation, possessed something of a glittering eye.

See "The Power of the Eye in Coleridge," by Lane Cooper, in *Studies in Language and Literature in Celebration of the Seventieth Birthday of James Morgan Hart*, 1910, pp. 78–121; reprinted in Cooper's *Late Harvest*, 1952.

9. The last two lines of this stanza were written by Wordsworth.

10. Spectators cheer as the ship leaves the harbor. The men are in a merry mood as they see vanish in the distance first the church, then a hill, finally the top of the lighthouse. Because the word "kirk" is used for "church" in Scotland and northern England, presumably the seaport is somewhere in this region.

The time of the voyage is also unspecified, though the archaic words

The Wedding-
Guest is
spellbound by
the eye of the old
seafaring man,
and constrained
to hear his tale.

He holds him with his glittering eye—**8**
The Wedding-Guest stood still,
And listens like a three years' child:
The Mariner hath his will.**9**

* The Wedding-Guest sat on a stone:
He cannot choose but hear;
And thus spake on that ancient man,
20   The bright-eyed Mariner.

The Mariner tells
how the ship
sailed southward
with a good
wind and fair
weather, till it
reached the line.

"The ship was cheered, the harbour
   cleared,
Merrily did we drop
Below the kirk, below the hill,
Below the lighthouse top.**10**

and many of the lines suggest a medieval period (see Note 34). The ship travels south across the Equator (always called the "line" in Coleridge's gloss), down past the coast of Brazil. A storm drives the ship into antarctic waters. After rounding Cape Horn, the southern-most promontory of South America, trade winds carry the ship north-ward through the Pacific to the Equator where it is becalmed. The precise course of the ship for the rest of the poem is not clear (see Note 119). Moved by occult forces, it presumably is carried south and west to round the Cape of Good Hope (the southern tip of Africa), then northward through Atlantic waters and back to home port.

This round-the-world cruise, with its two huge loops like a monstrous "W" wrapped around the globe, provides the basic framework of the narrative. In Coleridge's day it was a familiar framework. Many a ship had sailed along such a route, and many a book had been written about such a voyage. In particular, the loop around Cape Horn, from Atlantic to Pacific, had been tra-versed by ship after ship through-out the seventeenth and eighteenth centuries. At the time he wrote the poem, Coleridge was absorbed in reading accounts of just such voy-ages—his imagination, as Lowes expresses it, "playing like heat-lightning, about the remote hori-zons of the world."

"The basic structure of the voy-age," writes Lowes, ". . . is as true to fact as an Admiralty report . . . And now on this frame, as upon a loom, the imagination was to weave . . . a magic pattern. But the magic plays, like a strange light over a familiar landscape, upon a ground-work of fact deep-rooted as the continents themselves, and perme-ated with the elemental experience of humanity."

11. In other words, the ship heads south.

12. As one travels south toward the Equator, the sun at noon rises higher and higher in the sky. At the Equator, the noonday sun is never far from the zenith; during the autumnal and vernal equinoxes (September 23 and March 21) it is directly overhead. Whenever the poem speaks of the sun as over the mast at noon, it means that the ship is on the Equator.

As Lowes points out (Chap. IV) the main events of the poem occur when the ship is becalmed at the Equator in the Pacific. It would have blunted these events had Coleridge lingered over the voyage south to Cape Horn, so it is necessary for him to slide his ship rapidly through this first part of the loop around the Cape. "It is all as expeditious as a magic carpet," writes Lowes. "The vertical sun stands over the mast for an instant at noon, to mark the crossing of the Line. Then the dramatic incursion of the wedding revelry, like the knocking in *Macbeth*, snaps for a moment the spell of the tale, and, with the fine economy of a practiced art, blots the superfluous first passage of the tropics completely from the poem . . . That is the most superb *tour de force* in the poem . . ."

13. The tones of the bassoon, a double-reeded woodwind with a pitch lower than that of its cousin the oboe, foreshadow the subterranean, daemonic atmosphere of the Mariner's tale. The mention of a bassoon is one of the poem's anachronisms; musical instruments that can legitimately be called bassoons were not in existence before the sixteenth century, a fact that jars with evidence (see Note 34) that the poem's action takes place in the Middle Ages.

While Coleridge was working on *The Ancient Mariner,* the church choir at Stowey was given a bassoon by Coleridge's friend Thomas Poole, in whose house he was living. It has been suggested that this also may have influenced Coleridge's use of the instrument in this stanza.

14. Red as a rose: A simile used frequently in the old ballads. Robert Burns had earlier written, "O, my luve's like a red, red rose," but Coleridge's phrasing suggests that the bride is not only as beautiful as a rose, but also blushing the color of a rose. Note the contrast between the bride's complexion and the leprous white skin of the harlot in line 192.

15. Nodding: Nodding their heads in time to the music.

Minstrelsy: The musicians. Musicians nod in another Coleridge poem. The first line of the next-to-last stanza of "The Ballad of the Dark Ladié" reads: "But first the nodding minstrels go . . ."

The Sun came up upon the left,
Out of the sea came he!
And he shone bright, and on the right
Went down into the sea.**11**

Higher and higher every day,
30   Till over the mast at noon—"**12**
The Wedding-Guest here beat his breast,
For he heard the loud bassoon.**13**

The Wedding-
Guest heareth the
bridal music;
but the Mariner
continueth
his tale.

* The bride hath paced into the hall,
Red as a rose is she;**14**
Nodding their heads before her goes
The merry minstrelsy.**15**

16. Every line in this stanza repeats a previous line. This technique of repeating earlier lines and phrases is characteristic of the old English ballads Coleridge is imitating.

17. In *Sibylline Leaves* and later printings, the word "drawn" appears here instead of "driven." James Dykes Campbell, in his *Poetical Works of Samuel Taylor Coleridge,* made the change, and most critics, though not all, have accepted it. Campbell points out that the stanza speaks of the Storm-blast chasing the ship, and in earlier printings of the poem this line is: "Like chaff we drove along."

"Coleridge, I have no doubt," writes Campbell, "wrote *driven,* but in very small characters on the narrow margin of *Lyrical Ballads;* the word was misprinted *drawn,* and the mistake was overlooked then and after."

18. The basic stanza of Coleridge's poem employs the traditional ballad rhyme scheme, *abcb.* As Tristram P. Coffin makes clear (in his paper on "Coleridge's Use of the Ballad Stanza in 'The Rime of the Ancient Mariner' "), Coleridge carefully maintains the traditional stanza, to impress it firmly on the reader's mind, until he reaches this point where he introduces the first major variation. I quote from Coffin:

> What then happens when the poet breaks the established norm at this point? Is it purposeful, or is it, as Coleridge no doubt thought it to be in the native ballad, an inconsistency caused by the spontaneity of composition? The answer is that it is purposeful and serves to make more poignant for the reader the meaning of the words at this point.

By using an expansion of the stanza, which was quite common to the ballads he knew, consciously just as the ship is driven from the known course into the mystery of the polar regions, the author gently channels our ears and eyes away from the expected into a consistent, but different, realm, yet a realm that is never so vastly different that the basic pulse of the ballad beat is destroyed or the "anchor dislodged." Actually Stanza 12 remains an *abcb* stanza, but the triple reiteration of the *a*-rime line gives a fresh effect.

The word "still," in the stanza's third line, has the poetic meaning of always or continually.

19. The ship leans forward as the storm drives it south, like one who bends his head as he runs, but is so closely followed that he cannot escape from the shadow of the foe who pursues him. The tempestuous winds around Cape Horn are prominent in many of the travel books read by Coleridge. In the final line the word "aye" (rhymes with "say") is an archaism meaning "always" or "continually." "The swiftness and persistence of pursuit," writes the Chicago poet William Vaughn Moody in commenting on this stanza, "is echoed in the closer crowding of the rhymes."

20. All the phrases of this stanza (as Lowes makes abundantly clear in his chapter on "The Fields of Ice") are to be found in the arctic travel books that Coleridge read. The poet simply "reversed the poles," as Lowes puts it. "Ice is ice, be it austral or boreal waters in which it floats and howls—and anyway, none of his readers has ever been the wiser!"

One voyager writes, "whereupon followed mist and snow," and later, "the ice came floating down . . .

The ship driven **17** by a storm toward the south pole.

The Wedding-Guest he beat his breast,
Yet he cannot choose but hear;
And thus spake on that ancient man,
⁴⁰ The bright-eyed Mariner.**16**

"And now the Storm-blast came, and he
Was tyrannous and strong:
He struck with his o'ertaking wings,
And chased us south along.

With sloping masts and dipping prow,
As who pursued with yell and blow
Still treads the shadow of his foe,**18**
And forward bends his head,
* The ship drove fast, loud roared the blast,
⁵⁰ And southward aye we fled.**19**

* And now there came both mist and snow,
And it grew wondrous cold:
And ice, mast-high, came floating by,
As green as emerald.**20**

and it was very cold." Another writer repeatedly speaks of icebergs as high or higher than the ship's top-mast. The ice is commonly described as white or blue, but sometimes "of a pale green color." "Nor do their figures and shapes alone surprise," declares one voyager, "but also their diversity of colors . . . for some are like white crystal, others as blue as sapphires, and others again as green as emeralds."

"Has our confidence in the supreme originality of a work of genius been after all misplaced?" asks Lowes. "Well," he answers, "there is the stanza! Hunt till doomsday through Martens and Harris and Captain James, and you will not find it. The words are severally the words of the voyagers; the shining constellation of images—simple as kirk or hill, and clear as air—which rose out of their confluence, was the birth of a shaping brain that was not the travellers'. And the stanza bears Coleridge's image and superscription stamped on every line."

21. Ken: An archaic word here used in the sense of "saw."

22. In the first line of this stanza the word "drifts" means floating or drifting ice; it often has that sense in the eighteenth-century books about polar explorations. "Clifts," another word used repeatedly by the explorers, is synonymous with "clefts." The "snowy clifts" in the poem are huge fissures filled with snow.

The brilliant luster of the ice and snow was noted by all of the early polar voyagers. Lowes quotes many passages. The following is typical: "the snow was marbeled, and . . . gave as bright and glorious a shining or gloss to the air or skies, as if the sun had shined."

The writers also underlined the desolation of polar landscapes. In Shelvocke's *Voyage* (from which Coleridge took the incident of the albatross; see Note 25) the following lines appear: "The heavens were perpetually hid from us by gloomy, dismal clouds . . . One would think it impossible that any thing living could subsist in so rigid a climate; and, indeed, we . . . had not had the sign of one fish of any kind . . . nor one sea-bird, except a disconsolate black albatross."

The meaning of the stanza is clear. Between the gigantic, emerald-green icebergs, land can be seen: a desolate, lifeless land of snowy crevasses that give off a dismal sheen.

23. Lowes marshals a page or two of quotations, from the arctic travel books of the time, in which every verb in this line except "growled" is used to describe the terrifying sounds made by polar icebergs. One excerpt will here suffice: "There was such a frightful rumbling and cracking of the ice, as if many cannons had been fired at once, and then ensued a violent noise, like the roaring of a cascade."

24. "Swound" is an archaic word for "swoon." A person regaining consciousness, after having fainted, apparently experiences a sudden, jarring onrush of sounds. "I suppose I am offering a counsel of perfection," writes Lowes, "but if there is no other way, I am not at all sure that it is not well worth while to be knocked senseless (within reasonable limits), for the sake of the unique experience of coming to. At all events, nobody who has not come up through those bizarre and sinister noises is quite competent to catch the powerful suggestion of the simile."

A contemporary reviewer of *Lyrical Ballads* complained that the phrase "noises of a swound" was nonsensical. This may explain why, when the second edition appeared in 1800, Coleridge altered the line to "A wild and ceaseless sound." Later, he restored the original line except for the substitution of "in" for "of."

Was Coleridge aware of the portmanteau character of "swound," which suggests sound, wind, and wound as well as swoon?

25. It was Wordsworth who proposed to Coleridge that an albatross be brought into his ballad and that the shooting of the bird provide

The Rime of the Ancient Mariner from Coleridge's *Poetical Works*, 1834

The land of ice,
and of fearful
sounds where
no living thing
was to be seen.

And through the drifts the snowy clifts
Did send a dismal sheen:
Nor shapes of men nor beasts we ken—**21**
The ice was all between.**22**

* The ice was here, the ice was there,
The ice was all around:
It cracked and growled, and roared and
howled,**23**
Like noises in a swound!**24**

60

Till a great
sea-bird, called
the Albatross,
came through the
snow-fog, and
was received with
great joy and
hospitality.

At length did cross an Albatross,**25**
Through the fog it came;**26**
As if it had been a Christian soul,
We hailed it in God's name.

the Mariner's "crime." The idea had been suggested to Wordsworth by his reading of *A Voyage Round the World by the Way of the Great South Sea*, by Captain George Shelvocke, London, 1726. Shelvocke speaks of a "disconsolate black albatross" (see Note 22) that followed the ship for several days, "hovering about us as if he had lost himself, till Hatley, (my second captain) observing, in one of his melancholy fits, that this bird was always hovering near us, imagined, from his color, that it might be some ill omen. That which, I suppose, induced him the more to encourage his superstition, was the continued series of contrary tempestuous winds, which had oppressed us ever since we had got into the sea. But be that as it would, he, after some fruitless attempts, at length, shot the albatross, not doubting (perhaps) that we should have a fair wind after it."

Whether Coleridge did or did not read Shelvocke after Wordsworth mentioned the book, or whether he perhaps already had read it, is not decisively known. Lowes (who discusses this question in Note 18 to Chap. XIII of his book) is of the opinion that Coleridge *did* read Shelvocke, after Wordsworth had called the book to his attention, and he cites convincing evidence to support this view.

The most impressive of the various species of albatross is the Wandering Albatross of the southern seas; it is an enormous snow-white bird with jet-black wing tips, a long beak that hooks downward at the tip, and webbed feet like a duck. It is the largest of all sea birds. Its weight is fifteen to twenty-five pounds, and its wing spread ten to twelve feet, and sometimes longer. The bird travels alone and is capable of following a ship for days without resting on the water. At intervals it glides down to feed on refuse from the ship's galley and on squids and shrimps churned to the surface in the ship's wake.

"Bethink thee of the albatross," asks Herman Melville ("The Whiteness of the Whale," Chap. 42, *Moby Dick)* "whence come those clouds of spiritual wonderment and pale dread, in which that white phantom sails in all imaginations? Not Coleridge first threw that spell; but

God's great, unflattering laureate, Nature."

To this sentence Melville appends the following footnote:

I remember the first albatross I ever saw. It was during a prolonged gale, in waters hard upon the Antarctic seas. From my forenoon watch below, I ascended to the overclouded deck; and there, dashed upon the main hatches, I saw a regal, feathery thing of unspotted whiteness, and with a hooked, Roman bill sublime. At intervals, it arched forth its vast archangel wings, as if to embrace some holy ark. Wonderous flutterings and throbbings shook it. Though bodily unharmed, it uttered cries, as some king's ghost in supernatural distress. Through its inexpressible, strange eyes, methought I peeped to secrets which took hold of God. As Abraham before the angels, I bowed myself; the white thing was so white, its wings so wide, and in those for ever exiled waters, I had lost the miserable warping memories of traditions and of towns. Long I gazed at that prodigy of plumage. I cannot tell, can only hint, the things that darted through me then. But at last I awoke; and turning, asked a sailor what bird was this. A goney, he replied. Goney! I never had heard that name before; is it conceivable that this glorious thing is utterly unknown to men ashore! never! But some time after, I learned that goney was some seaman's name for albatross. So that by no possibility could Coleridge's wild Rhyme have had aught to do with those mystical impressions which were mine, when I saw that bird upon our deck. For neither had I then read the Rhyme, nor knew the bird to be an albatross. Yet, in saying this, I do but indirectly burnish a little brighter the noble merit of the poem and the poet.

I assert, then, that in the wonderous bodily whiteness of the bird chiefly lurks the secret of the spell; a truth the more evinced in this, that by a solecism of terms there are birds called gray albatrosses; and these I have frequently seen, but never with such emotions as when I beheld the Antarctic fowl.

But how had the mystic thing been caught? Whisper it not, and I will tell; with a treacherous hook and line, as the fowl floated on the sea. At last the Captain made a postman of it; tying a lettered, leathern tally round its neck, with the ship's time and place; and then letting it escape. But I doubt not, that leathern tally, meant for man, was taken off in Heaven, when the white fowl flew to join the wing-folding, the invoking, and adoring cherubim!

Was this the species of bird the Mariner shot? Lowes is not sure. The "black albatross" mentioned by Shelvocke was probably the Sooty Albatross, a species also plentiful in antarctic waters, but much smaller in size than the Wanderer. Coleridge nowhere specifies the color of the bird; that he may have had in mind the smaller, darker albatross is suggested by lines 67 and 142 (see Notes 27 and 55).

Albatrosses figure in numerous sea travel books of the time. Sailors regarded the bird with superstitious awe and sometimes maintained that albatrosses harbored the transmigrated souls of evil old sea captains. Before Coleridge wrote his ballad, sailors may often have looked upon the birds as good or evil omens, but apparently did not hesitate to trap and kill them, either for sheer sport, or to make tobacco pouches from their webbed feet, pipes from their hollow wing bones, hand muffs from their breasts, even huge paperclips from their beaks. A reader wishing more information can consult Captain William Jameson's recent book, *The Wandering Albatross* (reprinted in 1961 as a Doubleday Anchor paperback), or the many references listed in its bibliography.

26. Thorough: An archaic form of "through."

27. We know what sort of food the albatross ate—the food it never before had eaten—because this line originally was: "The Marineres gave it biscuit-worms."

In England a biscuit is what in the United States is called a cracker. Biscuit-worms are the maggots that infest old, deteriorating biscuits; there are many references to them in the sea travel books. Coleridge may have changed the line because of its offensiveness, or because he had learned for the first time of the huge size of the albatross (this assumes he did not have in mind the smaller Sooty Albatross; see Note 25) and realized the absurdity of having such a Brobdingnagian creature (as Lowes puts it) eat food suitable for a wren.

Coleridge may also have wished to suggest, by his revised line, that there had been no previous ships in the area. *Any* food the sailors gave the bird would be food of a type it never before had eaten.

28. Thunder-fit: Thunder clap.

29. "Good south wind" is a common phrase of the sea. The wind reverses the direction of the ship, starting it on its journey northward into the Pacific.

30. Hollo: A loud shout, traditional in English hunting. Writes Byron (in *Age of Bronze*): "The hounds will gather to their huntsman's hollo."

31. Shrouds are the heavy ropes that stretch from the top of the mast to the sides of the ship. They serve to keep the mast rigid.

32. Vespers are a Roman Catholic and Anglican prayer service held at sunset, but the word is here used in the more general sense of "vesper hours" or evenings. The "nine" does not mean nine o'clock, but that on nine evenings (*i.e.*, for nine days) at the vesper hour of twilight, the albatross roosted on the ship.

The perching of the bird on "mast or shroud" may be taken to suggest that it was no ordinary albatross, but more likely it reflects Coleridge's ignorance of albatrosses. The bird's three webbed toes face forward, with no toe behind, rendering it unable to perch on anything. However, in the poet's defense it should be added that sailors often brought back tales of albatrosses that rested on the ship's rigging.

33. The look of horror on the Mariner's face, as he recalls his crime, is powerfully implied by the Wedding-Guest's question. This indirect suggestion is a technique characteristic of old English ballads. Coleridge employs it with great skill in many places in his poem.

34. The cross-bow was a medieval weapon for shooting arrows, stones, and other missiles by means of a bow drawn back over a groove, with a trigger mechanism for holding and releasing the taut string. Its use by the Mariner is one of the ballad's strongest indications that the action probably takes place in the Middle Ages, or certainly not later than the sixteenth century, the last century in which crossbows were in common use. For other indications see Notes 42, 66, 84, 125, 146, 153. A medieval atmosphere is also conveyed by the constant use of archaic words. (See, however, Note 13.)

35. Coleridge supplies no reason for the shooting of the albatross,

* It ate the food it ne'er had eat,**27**
And round and round it flew.
The ice did split with a thunder-fit;**28**
70 The helmsman steered us through!

And lo! the Albatross proveth a bird of good omen, and followeth the ship as it returned northward through fog and floating ice.

And a good south wind sprung up behind;**29**
The Albatross did follow,
And every day, for food or play,
Came to the mariner's hollo!**30**

In mist or cloud, on mast or shroud,**31**
It perched for vespers nine;**32**
Whiles all the night, through fog-smoke white,
Glimmered the white Moon-shine."

The ancient Mariner inhospitably killeth the pious bird of good omen.

"God save thee, ancient Mariner!
From the fiends, that plague thee
80   thus!—
* Why look'st thou so?"**33**—With my cross-bow**34**
I shot the ALBATROSS.**35**

an omission that intensifies the incident's role as symbolic of the ultimate crime, the crime of murder. Apparently the shooting was a premeditated, wanton act of cruelty. In an earlier (1800) printing of *Lyrical Ballads,* the "Argument" at the head of the poem speaks of "how the Ancient Mariner cruelly and in contempt of the laws of hospitality killed a Seabird . . ." The cruelty is heightened by the friendly behavior of the "pious bird," its apparent influence in splitting the ice and bringing the "good south wind," and by the fact (brought out later in Line 404) that the bird loved the Mariner.

Note how startling and effective is the technique of ending Part I with a simple, abrupt statement of the crime.

PART II

36. The ship, having rounded the Cape, is now sailing north.

37. 'Em: Coleridge is not lapsing here into colloquialism. The ancestor of "them" was "hem," often spelled in this contracted form.

38. The sea travel books read by Coleridge contain many references to the sudden, welcome appearance of the sun after weary months of sailing through polar fog. One writer even calls it "the glorious sun." The likening of the sun to the head of God offended at least one contemporary reviewer; he wrote that the simile "makes a reader shudder, not with poetic feeling, but with religious disapprobation." Such criticism probably prompted Coleridge to alter the phrase (in the 1800 edition of *Lyrical Ballads*) to "like an Angel's head," but for the 1802 edition he had the courage to restore his original words.

Coleridge speaks of a "glorious sun" in his poem "This Lime-tree Bower My Prison," and again in "Fears in Solitude" where the phrase is clearly a symbol of God. After deploring the decay of genuine religious faith in England, while everyone simultaneously professes to be a Christian, the following well-known lines occur:

> All, all make up one scheme of
> perjury,
> That faith doth reel; the very name
> of God
> Sounds like a juggler's charm; and,
> bold with joy,
> Forth from his dark and lonely
> hiding-place,
> (Portentous sight!) the owlet
> Atheism,
> Sailing on obscene wings athwart
> the noon,

> Drops his blue-fringed lids, and
> holds them close,
> And hooting at the glorious sun in
> Heaven,
> Cries out, "Where is it?"

The reference to "dim and red," which the glorious sun was not, anticipates the "bloody sun" in line 112, a sun of vengeance that marks the beginning of the crew's punishment for the bloody crime. R. C. Bald has pointed out that in one of his notebooks Coleridge refers to having read a set of sermons by Robert South. One of these sermons, on the Resurrection, speaks of Christ as a "sun of righteousness" with a "glorious rising, after a red and bloody setting," but one can only guess whether this passage influenced Coleridge's line.

Uprist: uprose.

39. Note that the gloss for this stanza gives information unobtainable from the poem itself; namely that by justifying the killing of the albatross, the shipmates become accomplices in the crime. Many of Coleridge's later marginal comments supply information either not in the poem at all, or at best obtained from the poem only by highly speculative deduction. (For example: the becalming of the ship begins the avenging of the crime, the Mariner's guardian saint sends down the angelic troop, the polar daemon obeys the angels, and many other significant details.)

B. R. McElderry, Jr., in his valuable article on "Coleridge's Revision of 'The Ancient Mariner,'" points out that when the poem was first printed it was heavily criticized for its obscurity. Many of Coleridge's revisions in 1800 were designed to make the poem more intel-

PART II

The Sun now rose upon the right:
Out of the sea came he,
Still hid in mist, and on the left
Went down into the sea.**36**

And the good south wind still blew be-
hind,
But no sweet bird did follow,
Nor any day for food or play
90 Came to the mariners' hollo!

His shipmates
cry out against
the ancient
Mariner, for
killing the bird
of good luck.

* And I had done a hellish thing,
And it would work 'em woe:**37**
For all averred, I had killed the bird
That made the bleeze to blow.
Ah wretch! said they, the bird to slay,
That made the breeze to blow!

But when the
fog cleared off,
they justify the
same, and thus
make themselves 100
accomplices in
the crime.

Nor dim nor red, like God's own head,
The glorious Sun uprist:**38**
Then all averred, I had killed the bird
That brought the fog and mist.
'Twas right, said they, such birds to
slay,
That bring the fog and mist.**39**

ligible. When he added the gloss in 1817, McElderry thinks he was not only attempting to make the text even clearer, but also that many of the ideas in the gloss were after-thoughts—thoughts not present in his mind when he first wrote the poem. If so, the addition of the gloss justifies, to a certain extent, the early criticism. It also may explain why certain obscurities remain. For example, the difficulty of knowing the exact movement of the ship after its becalming (see Note 119) may be due to the fact that Coleridge found himself un-able, when he prepared his gloss, to work out a coherent pattern for the ship's movements.

Note how line 101 repeats, with ironic effect, the words and phras-ing of line 95.

40. The easterly trade winds, which carry the ship northeast, were called "the Brises" in Coleridge's time. In the first version of the poem the line reads, "the breezes blew . . ."; contemporary readers would immediately take this as a reference to what are now called the trade winds. "The lost point of the line is worth retrieving," writes Lowes, because it reminds us that Coleridge always had in the back of his head an actual voyage around the Cape.

To his discussion of all this, Lowes appends a memorable footnote:

It is here, at last, that I can count with absolute assurance on some exasperated reader who will say: "But, in the name of all the unities and the proprieties at once, isn't this a fairy-tale? And what under the vertical sun and the hornèd moon has rigorous exactitude to do with the charting of seas beneath which polar dæmons lurk, and on which spectre-barks appear and vanish?" Such seas, we may own, they undoubtedly are. But mystery is then tenfold mysterious when it comes upon us out of the fixed and definite, and unfolds against the background of the surely known. And Coleridge's art is nowhere more supreme than in his scrupulous adherence to tangible fact in his universe of sheer imagination. And anyway, who of us dare lay a magisterial finger on the evanescent point at which the sea's tangible realities melt into its eternal, impalpable, brooding mystery? As for Coleridge, he, at least, was aware that haunted seas have trade winds—or that the seas swept by the trades are haunted, as you please.

41. This line has an amusing history. In the 1817 printing of his poem, Coleridge changed the line to: "The furrow stream'd off free."

In a footnote, Coleridge explained that the line had formerly been "The furrow follow'd free," then he added: "But I had not been long on board a ship, before I perceived that this was the image as seen by a spectator from the shore, or from another vessel. From the ship itself, the *Wake* appears like a brook flowing off from the stern."

Unfortunately, the new line lacked the pleasant alliteration of the original. When it was time for a new edition of *Sibylline Leaves,* Coleridge had decided that the poetry was more important than consistency in his frame of reference, so he restored the original line. For a more serious mistake involving the location of an observer, see Note 145.

42. Because Magellan, in 1520, was the first to burst into the Pacific, these lines suggest that the poem's action did not take place later than 1520. The two familiar lines are often quoted to emphasize a sudden encounter with something new and strange. I cite only one instance. In the last chapter of *Memories and Studies,* William James makes an eloquent plea for his "pluralistic universe," a universe whose history is not predetermined, but flavored with genuine novelty and wildness. "Every moment of immediate experience," he writes, "is somewhat absolutely original and novel." And then he quotes Coleridge's lines with an alteration of two words: "We are the first that ever burst into this silent sea."

43. Note how the slower movements of the lines of this stanza contrast with the fast moving lines of the previous one. The word

The fair breeze
continues; the
ship enters the
Pacific Ocean,
and sails
northward, even
till it reaches
the Line.

The fair breeze blew, the white foam**40**
   flew,
The furrow followed free;**41**
We were the first that ever burst
Into that silent sea.**42**

Down dropt the breeze, the sails dropt
   down,
'Twas sad as sad could be;
And we did speak only to break

The ship hath   **110**
been suddenly
becalmed.

The silence of the sea!**43**

All in a hot and copper sky,
The bloody Sun, at noon,
Right up above the mast did stand,
No bigger than the Moon.**44**

Day after day, day after day,
We stuck, nor breath nor motion;
As idle as a painted ship
Upon a painted ocean.

And the Albatross
begins to be   **120**
avenged.

* Water, water, every where,
And all the boards did shrink;**45**
Water, water, every where,
Nor any drop to drink.**46**

"break" was sometimes pronounced "breek" in Coleridge's day, and thus could rhyme with "speak" in the same line.

44. In several passages of Thomas Burnet's *Sacred Theory of the Earth* (see Note 1 on the epigraph) there are lurid descriptions of a "bloody sun." Lowes thinks that these passages are reflected in the first two lines of this stanza. The fact that the red sun is above the mast at noon indicates that the ship is becalmed at the Equator (see Note 12).

45. The absence of rain causes the ship's planks to shrink and warp. (Cf., line 529.)

46. The stanza's last two lines are surely the most often quoted, as well as the most often misquoted, lines in the ballad.

47. Lowes (Chap. V) offers convincing evidence that Coleridge found his rotting sea in the travel books he read: "viscous and glutinous water," says one writer, "some parts of the sea seemed covered with a kind of slime," says another, and so on. One writer devotes an entire chapter to various types of small fish that he calls "slime-fish." Concerning one variety, the "snail slime-fish," he says: "The seamen take these small fish for spiders . . . They swim in great numbers in the sea, as numerous as the dust in the sun." The star-fish is later described as having legs "like unto the feet of a spider."

"From that amazing carnival of miniature monsters," writes Lowes, "Coleridge, with an artistic restraint which must none the less have cast a longing look behind, seized upon the one touch which for sheer uncanny realism is unsurpassed: 'Yea, slimy things did crawl *with legs* upon a slimy sea.'"

48. About, about: Coleridge is quoting from a chant of the three witches in *Macbeth* (Act I, scene 3, lines 32–34):

> The weird sisters, hand in hand,
> Posters of the sea and land,
> Thus do go about, about.

The chant occurs just after one of the witches has pronounced a curse on a mariner, depriving him of drink and sleep, and sending a storm to wreck his ship.

49. Reel: A lively dance, chiefly associated with the Scottish reel. Also, a whirling movement.

Rout: The precise meaning here is hard to pin down because the word has been used in so many different senses. Coleridge probably had in mind a confused, disorganized state, like that of a fleeing mob.

50. "Death-fires" are ghostly lights, resembling will-o'-the-wisps, which the superstitious in Coleridge's day believed were often seen at night hovering over burial grounds. The light was supposed to come from decaying corpses. The fact is that rotting substances *do* sometimes glow in darkness. Decaying logs are often covered with luminous fungi that shine at night if you break the wood apart. The Roman writer Pliny, in the first century, speaks of "the luminescence of the trunk of the oak when it has become rotten with old age." Putrescent fish and the decaying bodies of animals (including humans) are sometimes attacked by luminous bacteria that emit a blue or blue-green glow. These facts undoubtedly entered into Coleridge's choice of the word "rot" in the previous stanza.

It is known that Coleridge had read Joseph Priestley's *Opticks*, a chapter of which is devoted to "Light from Putrescent Substances." Lowes argues convincingly (Chapter V, Sec. 2) that Coleridge's "death fires" are a fusion of graveyard fires, St. Elmo's fire (an electrostatic glow that at times surrounds prominent points on a ship), and the general bioluminescence of the sea. (For an excellent, up-to-date survey of what science knows about bioluminescence, see the article "Biological Luminescence," by William D. McElroy and Howard H. Seliger, in *Scientific American*, November, 1962.)

In an earlier poem, "Ode to the Departing Year," Coleridge had

The very deep did rot: O Christ!
That ever this should be!
Yea, slimy things did crawl with legs
Upon the slimy sea.**47**

* About, about,**48** in reel and rout**49**
The death-fires danced at night;**50**
The water, like a witch's oils,
130   Burnt green, and blue and white.**51**

used the image of dancing death-fires:

> Mighty armies of the dead
> Dance, like death-fires, round her
> tomb!

51. As every seafaring man knows, the ocean's surface swarms with minute animal and plant life known collectively as plankton. They are the "pastures of the sea," and become food for the smallest fish, which in turn are eaten by larger fish, and so on down the ocean's gulp-order. Many plankton organisms are luminescent, especially when agitated. This explains the brilliant, glowing white foam that churns up at night along the sides of moving ships, and gives to the wake its milky luminescence. When waves at night are high enough for the crests to break, the turbulence produces a similar glow. The voyagers, whose books Coleridge read, often spoke of such luminescence as a kind of "burning." "At times, when the sea dasheth very much," reads one passage (I quote, as usual, from Lowes), "it shines like fire, the seamen call it burning."

Even when the sea dasheth not, its rippling surface often glows with a pale fire. At times, the fire is tinged with color—most often, but not always, blue. Lowes cites a passage, from Captain James Cook's *Voyage to the Pacific Ocean,* in which Cook speaks of white, blue, and green luminescence, precisely the three colors that are in Coleridge's line. Lowes sees in the last two lines of this stanza a merging of the witches' oils (from the weird sisters of *Macbeth*) with the colors in Captain Cook's description.

This has an interest beyond that of merely finding probable sources for Coleridge's imagery; it indicates that the stanza was not intended as sheer fantasy. Like the one before it, it describes a scene—albeit exaggerated and dramatized—which Coleridge firmly believed to be sober factual reporting.

Witch's oils: Mysterious oils that burn with vivid colors, and are supposedly used by witches in the preparation of their charms.

52. Assuréd were: Were given a revelation.

53. The Spirit haunting the ship, and fellow daemons who enter the ballad later, are not demonic in the Jewish or Christian sense of devils or fallen angels, but *daemonic* in the sense made clear in the gloss. Like unfallen angels, they are intelligent beings on a higher plane of existence than man (see the poem's epigraph). (Consult Lowes, Chap. XIII, Sec. 4, for a discussion of the Neoplatonic literature from which Coleridge fished his water daemon.)

54. Well a-day!: Alas! This was a common exclamation in old English ballads.

55. Many commentators have pointed out that the Wandering Albatross is too large a bird to be hung around a sailor's neck. Lowes quotes from Hawthorne's *English Note Books* a passage in which Hawthorne tells of visiting a museum "rich in specimens of ornithology, among which was an albatross, huge beyond imagination. I do not think Coleridge could have known the size of the fowl when he caused it to be hung round the neck of the Ancient Mariner."

Coleridge may have had in mind a smaller species of albatross, some of which are no larger than geese, or the bird may have been a Wanderer, and in spite of its weight and size, hung on the Mariner anyway. Its wings could have been cut off, or allowed to trail the deck.

The phrase "instead of a cross" suggests that the Mariner, whom we know to be a Roman Catholic, had been wearing on his neck a cross. Perhaps his shipmates had removed it because they believed he no longer deserved to wear it. Lowes thinks there may also be a suggestion here of the mark of the cross said to have been branded on the forehead of the Wandering Jew. (See Note 170.)

A Spirit had followed them; one of the invisible inhabitants of this planet, neither departed souls nor angels; concerning whom the learned Jew, Josephus, and the Platonic Constantinopolitan, Michael Psellus, may be consulted. They are very numerous, and there is no climate or element without one or more.

And some in dreams assuréd were**52**
Of the Spirit that plagued us so;
* Nine fathom deep he had followed us
From the land of mist and snow.**53**

The shipmates, in their sore distress, would fain throw the whole guilt on the ancient Mariner: in sign whereof they hang the dead sea-bird round his neck.

140

And every tongue, through utter drought,
Was withered at the root;
We could not speak, no more than if
We had been choked with soot.

Ah! well a-day! what evil looks**54**
Had I from old and young!
Instead of the cross, the Albatross
About my neck was hung.**55**

PART III

56. This entire stanza first appeared in the *Sibylline Leaves* printing of the ballad. Note how effectively the four repetitions of "weary" add to the feeling of weariness conveyed by the stanza.
57. Wist: Knew.
58. Tacked: Turned toward the wind. Veered: Turned away from the wind.

PART III

There passed a weary time. Each throat
Was parched, and glazed each eye.
A weary time! a weary time!
How glazed each weary eye,
When looking westward, I beheld
A something in the sky.**56**

The ancient
Mariner
beholdeth a sign
in the element
afar off.

¹⁵⁰

At first it seemed a little speck,
And then it seemed a mist;
It moved and moved, and took at last
A certain shape, I wist.**57**

* A speck, a mist, a shape, I wist!
And still it neared and neared:
As if it dodged a water-sprite,
It plunged and tacked and veered.**58**

61

59. The Mariner's throat is so dry that he is unable to speak until he has moistened his throat with blood. Note how the labials in this and the first line focus attention on the lips.

60. Gramercy!: In France today, this expression is equivalent to "Thank you" (from the Old French, *grant merci,* which originally meant "May God reward you"). Coleridge, however, uses it simply as an exclamation of great surprise, similar to "Mercy on us!" Samuel Johnson had given it that meaning in his dictionary, in 1755, and it was so used by later English writers.

61. Coleridge discloses (in *Table Talk,* entry for May 31, 1830) that the phrase "for joy did grin" was based upon a remark by a friend. In 1794 Coleridge and three companions had climbed to the top of Plinlimmon, a mountain in North Wales and "were nearly dead with thirst." "We could not speak from the constriction," Coleridge continues, "till we found a little puddle under a stone. He said to me: 'You grinned like an idiot!' He had done the same."

62. They drew in their breath as *if* they were drinking water.

63. Weal: Well-being, happiness, as in the familiar phrase "weal or woe." The ship no longer tacks from side to side on its way to do them good. Instead, it moves toward them, on even keel, without the help of wind or tide. Such phantom ships, propelled by unseen forces, figure in countless sea legends throughout the world. (See Lowes, Chap. XV, Sec. 3.)

64. A setting sun, its light refracted through dense layers of atmosphere, often assumes a broad oval-shape.

65. Flecked: Used here in the sense of striped.

66. The references to the Virgin Mary, here and in line 294, suggest a pre-Reformation date for the action. The Mariner may, of course, be a post-Reformation Roman Catholic, but in view of Coleridge's Protestant sentiments, together with suggestions in the ballad that the action takes place in the Middle Ages (see Note 34), the first interpretation seems preferable.

67. Gossameres: Filmy cobwebs that float in the air when the weather is calm. "Let even the restless gossamer / Sleep on the moveless air!" (Shelley, *Queen Mab.*)

At its nearer
approach, it
seemeth him to
be a ship; and
at a dear ransom
he freeth his
speech from the
bonds of thirst.   160

> With throats unslaked, with black lips
>   baked,
> We could nor laugh nor wail;
> Through utter drought all dumb we
>   stood!
> I bit my arm, I sucked the blood,**59**
> And cried, A sail! a sail!

> With throats unslaked, with black lips
>   baked,
> Agape they heard me call:
> Gramercy!**60** they for joy did grin,**61**
> And all at once their breath drew in,
> As they were drinking all.**62**

A flash of joy;

And horror
follows. For can
it be a ship that
comes onward
without wind
or tide?   170

> See! see! (I cried) she tacks no more!
> Hither to work us weal;**63**
> Without a breeze, without a tide,
> She steadies with upright keel!

> The western wave was all a-flame.
> The day was well nigh done!
> Almost upon the western wave
> Rested the broad bright Sun;**64**
> When that strange shape drove suddenly
> Betwixt us and the Sun.

It seemeth him
but the skeleton
of a ship.

  180

> And straight the Sun was flecked with
>   bars,**65**
> (Heaven's Mother send us grace!)**66**
> As if through a dungeon-grate he peered
> With broad and burning face.

And its ribs are
seen as bars
on the face of the
setting Sun.

> Alas! (thought I, and my heart beat
>   loud)
> How fast she nears and nears!
> Are those *her* sails that glance in
>   the Sun,
> Like restless gossameres?**67**

68. A Death: A skeleton. Death is traditionally personified as a skeleton figure. At first the Mariner wonders if other skeletons are on the ship; then he realizes that the skeleton is Death itself.

69. The skeleton ship, with its gruesome pair, resembles in many ways a spectre ship in an old Dutch sea tale that may have reached Coleridge's ears. In this legend a murderer named Falkenberg is doomed to wander until judgment day on a crewless ship, while two spectral figures—one black, one white—dice for his soul (see Lowes, Chap. XV, Sec. 3). Note that Coleridge's female figure, Life-in-Death, has leprous white skin, and her husband, Death, is (in a stanza that appeared in the poem's first version) a jet-black skeleton.

In a copy of the 1798 edition of *Lyrical Ballads,* Coleridge added in the margin, at this spot, another stanza—one which never appeared in any of the ballad's printings:

> This ship it was a plankless thing,
> —A bare Anatomy!
> A plankless Spectre—and it mov'd
> Like a being of the Sea!
> The woman and a fleshless man
> Therein sate merrily.

70. Why the italics in this line? In the original version of the ballad the harlot, Death-in-life, is pictured in sharp contrast to the black skeleton of Death, so Coleridge may have intended the italics to stress the differences between the two, but it is puzzling that Coleridge did not remove the italics when he excised the stanza describing Death. Almost as mystifying is the use of italicized "hers" in reference to the spectre ship in the two previous stanzas. It seems unlikely that they are mistakes. Perhaps they were designed to stress the Mariner's difficulty in believing that he actually does see the sails and body of a ship.

The word "free" suggests that the woman's expression, like that of a tart seeking trade, is overfree, unrestrained, licentious. The two figures may have been influenced by Milton's horrendous account (*Paradise Lost,* Book II) of the mating of Sin with her own son (by Satan), the shapeless black monster Death.

Elliott B. Gose, Jr., in his article on "Coleridge and the Luminous Gloom" (*Publications of the Modern Language Association of America,* June, 1960) makes an interesting observation. The sun, which he takes as a God-symbol, is normally yellow in color, but in its bloody red form symbolizes God's wrath. The same two colors are here applied to the harlot: "a frightful parody of the life-giving colors associated with the sun whose place she has temporarily usurped."

71. R. L. Brett points out, in *Reason and Imagination* (Oxford, 1960), that Coleridge undoubtedly intended a vivid contrast here between the whiteness of the skin of the harlot Life-in-Death and the rosy complexion of the bride—an obvious symbol of life—in line 34. Brett writes: "This is the great contrast underlying the whole poem: on the one hand life; on the other the life-in-death that follows on separation from God. These form the axis around which the poem turns."

The Rime of the Ancient Mariner from Coleridge's *Poetical Works*, 1834

The Spectre-Woman and her Death-mate, and no other on board the skeleton ship.

Are those *her* ribs through which the Sun
Did peer, as through a grate?
And is that Woman all her crew?
Is that a DEATH? and are there two?**68**
Is DEATH that woman's mate?**69**

Like vessel, ¹⁹⁰
like crew!

Her lips were red, *her* looks were free,**70**
Her locks were yellow as gold:
Her skin was as white as leprosy,**71**
The Night-mare LIFE-IN-DEATH was she,**72**
Who thicks man's blood with cold.

Death and Life-in-Death have diced for the ship's crew, and she (the latter) winneth the ancient Mariner.

The naked hulk alongside came,**73**
And the twain were casting dice;
* "The game is done! I've won! I've won!"**74**
Quoth she, and whistles thrice.**75**

72. Night-mare: The hyphenated spelling better conveys the original meaning of the word. I quote from the *Oxford English Dictionary:* "A female spirit or monster supposed to beset people and animals by night, settling upon them when they are asleep and producing a feeling of suffocation by its weight."

Shortly before his death, a hopeless dope addict and semi-invalid, Coleridge looked back on his years of unrequited love and unfulfilled dreams, and thought of his own life as a nightmare life-in-death. This is how he wrote his own epitaph:

> Stop, Christian passer-by!—Stop, child of God,
> And read with gentle breast. Beneath this sod
> A poet lies, or that which once seem'd he.
> O lift one thought in prayer for S. T. C.;
> That he who many a year with toil of breath

Found death in life, may here find life in death!
Mercy for praise—to be forgiven for fame
He ask'd, and hoped, through Christ. Do thou the same!

73. Naked hulk: A hulk without planking.

74. Death wins all the crew except the Mariner. The Mariner's doom is to live on in a kind of suspended animation, unable to die (cf., line 262), surrounded by the bodies of his dead shipmates.

75. In the poem's first version, the whistling of Life-in-Death is followed by a whistling of the wind through the bones, eye sockets, and mouth of the skeleton Death. This stanza of pure Gothic horror was later removed by Coleridge. Apparently he wanted to leave the image of Death more to the reader's imagination, and at the same time eliminate a passage that contemporary readers had found offensively hideous.

76. The absence of twilight in the tropics—the quickness with which stars rush out and cold night follows hot day—was proverbial in Coleridge's time. Here the poet couples it with the speed of the departing spectre ship.

The stanza's gloss had an interesting evolution (see Lowes, Chap. X, Sec. 4). In the first edition of *Sibylline Leaves* (containing the first printing of the poem with a marginal gloss), the margin beside this stanza is blank. But there exist several copies of *Sibylline Leaves* in which Coleridge added notes to this stanza. The earliest reads: "Between the tropics there is no twilight. As the sun's last segment dips down, and the evening-gun is fired, the constellations appear arrayed."

A later note: "No twilight where there is no latitude nor yet on either side within the park and race-course of the sun." And still later: "Within the tropics there is no twilight. At the moment, the *second,* that the sun sinks, the stars appear all at once as if at the word of command announced by the evening gun, in our W. India Islands."

When *Sibylline Leaves* was reprinted in 1828, Coleridge used the simple, effective sentence that he had eleven years earlier written in a gift copy of the book: "No twilight within the courts of the sun."

77. In the ballad's first version, the ship leaves "with never a whisper." By changing this to "far-heard whisper," Coleridge emphasizes the sea's unearthly silence.

78. Fear drains blood from the Mariner's heart the way one drains a cup. Note how effectively the phrase "looked sideways up" conveys the fear on the sailors' faces.

79. At night, a lamp near the helmsman is necessary to illuminate the compass by which he steers.

80. Clomb: Climbed.

81. Eastern bar: The eastern horizon.

82. It has often been pointed out that this stanza seems to describe two events which could not possibly occur: (1) the appearance of a star within the tips of a crescent moon, (2) the rising of a new moon at sunset. Many critics have assumed that Coleridge intended both events to counter the laws of nature, thereby enhancing the supernatural atmosphere of his ballad; or perhaps he intended the impossible events to be the delusions of a crazed seaman dying of thirst. It is not so simple.

First, the star. Originally the line read "almost atween the tips." Such stars are, of course, common enough. Coleridge records in a notebook, before he altered the line, that he had seen a crescent moon with a star *touching* its tip. Later he changed the line to "Within the nether tip." A note he added to a copy of *Lyrical Ballads* reads: "It is a common superstition among sailors, 'that something evil is about to happen, whenever a star dogs the moon.'" Did Coleridge intend his star-dogged moon to violate natural law?

There is ample evidence he did not. The journals he read contain many references to the observation of strange lights, like stars, on the dark part of the moon. Lowes (Chap. XI, Sec. 3) cites many such references, beginning with Cotton

No twilight
within the courts   200
of the Sun.

The Sun's rim dips; the stars rush out:
At one stride comes the dark;**76**
With far-heard whisper, o'er the sea,**77**
Off shot the spectre-bark.

At the rising of
the Moon,

We listened and looked sideways up!
Fear at my heart, as at a cup,
My life-blood seemed to sip!**78**
The stars were dim, and thick the night,
The steersman's face by his lamp
   gleamed white;**79**
From the sails the dew did drip—
Till clomb**80** above the eastern bar**81**
210   The hornéd Moon, with one bright star
Within the nether tip.**82**

Mather's report that in Boston, November, 1668, "a star appeared below the body of the moon within the horns of it." Similar observations communicated by England's Astronomer Royal, Nevil Maskelyne, appeared in *Philosophical Transactions,* of the Royal Society of London, three years before *The Ancient Mariner* was written. Today's astronomers view these old reports with skepticism, but in Coleridge's time they were widely accepted and often taken as evidence for lunar volcanic activity. There is little doubt that Coleridge, reading of such observations, did not intend his star-dogged moon to be a supernatural event, but merely an extraordinary one.

As for the rising of a new moon at sunset, it is true that this cannot occur. A crescent moon is close to the sun. It rises in broad daylight and is well on its way toward setting by the time night comes on. But there is no reason to suppose

that Coleridge's moon rose at sunset. As Lowes makes clear, the stanza itself suggests a passage of time between sunset and the moon's appearance. The man at the helm steers the ship, his face white in the lamplight. The limp sails drip with dew. The next word, "Till," surely permits most of the night to slip by. It is a *dying* moon that rises in the east, *ahead* of the sun. "There *is* no blunder," concludes Lowes, who backs up his reasoning with quotations from his Harvard colleague, astronomer Harlow Shapley. "It is we who have been stupid, and not he [Coleridge]."

One moon problem remains. If this is a dying moon, it would not be possible, one week later (see line 261), for the moon to be as full and bright as it apparently is throughout the latter half of Part IV. Lowes concedes the discrepancy, but thinks it strengthens the poem's dreamlike distortion of the passage of time.

One after another,

One after one, by the star-dogged Moon,
Too quick for groan or sigh,
* Each turned his face with a ghastly
    pang,
And cursed me with his eye.

His shipmates
drop down dead.

Four times fifty living men,
  (And I heard nor sigh nor groan)
With heavy thump, a lifeless lump,
They dropped down one by one.**83**

But Life-in-Death 220
begins her work
on the ancient
Mariner.

The souls did from their bodies fly,—
They fled to bliss or woe!
And every soul, it passed me by,
Like the whizz of my cross-bow!**84**

83. The repetition of "one by one" (cf., line 212) suggests that one at a time each sailor stares at the dying moon, turns his eyes upon the Mariner, and drops lifeless to the deck.

84. Note how every section of the ballad ends with an allusion to the killing of the albatross. Here the death of each shipmate reminds the Mariner of his crime. The conception of the soul as a spiritual substance that left the body at death was common in the Middle Ages.

The Wedding-
Guest feareth
that a Spirit is
talking to him;

"I fear thee, ancient Mariner!
I fear thy skinny hand!
And thou art long, and lank, and brown,
As in the ribbed sea-sand.**85**

I fear thee and thy glittering eye,
And thy skinny hand, so brown."—
Fear not, fear not, thou Wedding-Guest!
This body dropt not down.

But the ancient   230
Mariner assureth
him of his
bodily life, and
proceedeth to
relate his
horrible pennance.

PART IV

85. In *Sibylline Leaves* Coleridge added here the following footnote: "For the last two lines of this stanza, I am indebted to Mr. Wordsworth. It was on a delightful walk from Nether Stowey to Dulverton, with him and his sister, in the Autumn of 1797, that this poem was planned, and in part composed."

Ribbed sea-sand: The Mariner's wrinkled skin resembles furrowed sea sand. Tides on sandy beaches leave ripples in the sand, but Wordsworth may have had a different sort of ribbing in mind. According to Ernest Hartley Coleridge ("The Genesis of the Ancient Mariner," *Poetry Review,* January, 1918), the beach at Kilve, where Wordsworth and Coleridge often went, is ribbed with bars of dark shale that emerge from the sand "like the spiny backs of a half-buried sea monster."

85a. Thomas Wolfe, while working on the novel that eventually was called *Look Homeward Angel,* wrote in 1927 to his former school-teacher, Margaret Roberts:

> I think I shall call it "Alone, Alone," for the idea that broods over it, and in it, and behind it is that we are all strangers upon this earth we walk on—that naked and alone do we come into life, and alone, a stranger, each to each, we live upon it. The title, as you know, I have taken from the poem I love best, "The Rime of the Ancient Mariner."

Wolfe then quotes the stanza to which this is a note. At Harvard, Wolfe had studied under John Livingston Lowes, before the publication of *The Road to Xanadu.* Lowes's belief that Coleridge's creative genius had fed unconsciously on memories acquired by prodigious reading had much to do with Wolfe's insane attempt, as a student, to read all the books in the Harvard library. Wolfe wrote a thesis for Lowes on "The Supernatural in the Poetry and Philosophy of Coleridge," and his discovery of a possible source for line 268 of *The Ancient Mariner* ("Like April hoar-frost spread") is cited in Chap. XII, Note 43 of Lowes's book.

86. See Note 47. In the next line the Mariner includes himself among the "slimy things."

87. Cf., line 123.

88. Or: Ere.

89. The imperfect rhyme (gusht, dust) may have resulted from Coleridge's inability to find a better one, or he may have chosen it deliberately; the halting rhyme does suggest the Mariner's halting efforts to pray.

Alone, alone, all, all alone,
Alone on a wide wide sea!
 * And never a saint took pity on
My soul in agony.**85a**

90. "The long-drawn third line gives an impression of weariness," said William Vaughn Moody of this stanza, "which is increased by retarding the stanza with an extra line and rhyme-word."

91. Although I have found no evidence to support this, it is plausible to suppose that among the superstitious in eighteenth-century England—or perhaps Coleridge is thinking of a medieval superstition—an orphan's curse, like the curse of an old person, a dying person, a priest, a beggar, and so on, was regarded as unusually potent.

The Rime of the Ancient Mariner from Coleridge's *Poetical Works*, 1834

He despiseth the
creatures of
the calm,

The many men, so beautiful!
And they all dead did lie:
And a thousand thousand slimy things**86**
Lived on; and so did I.

240   * I looked upon the rotting sea,**87**
And drew my eyes away;
I looked upon the rotting deck,
And there the dead men lay.

And envieth that
they should live,
and so many
lie dead.

I looked to heaven, and tried to pray;
But or ever a prayer had gusht,**88**
A wicked whisper came, and made
My heart as dry as dust.**89**

I closed my lids, and kept them close,
And the balls like pulses beat;
For the sky and the sea, and the sea and
250   the sky**90**
Lay like a load on my weary eye,
And the dead were at my feet.

But the curse
liveth for him in
the eye of the
dead men.

The cold sweat melted from their limbs,
Nor rot nor reek did they:
The look with which they looked on me
Had never passed away.

An orphan's curse would drag to hell**91**
A spirit from on high;
But oh! more horrible than that
260   Is the curse in a dead man's eye!
  * Seven days, seven nights, I saw that
      curse,
And yet I could not die.

92. The rising of the moon in this marvelous stanza, with its equally marvelous gloss, may signify the easing of the Mariner's harsh punishment. The isolation and horror that occurred under the "bloody sun" now gives way to penance and redemption under the moon. As J. B. Beer points out (in *Coleridge the Visionary*) the reference to "a star or two beside" is clearly intended to sharpen the contrast between *this* moon, a symbol of reconciliation, and the moon dogged by a star *within* its crescent, a symbol of daemonic vengeance.

93. Main: Sea. The moon's beams "bemock" in the sense that her cold frosty light seems contemptuous of the sultry sea.

94. "For the shadows that the moon casts are strange, and not like other shadows . . ." So wrote T. Page Wright, a motion-picture writer, at the beginning of the epigraph for his one book of poems, *Shadows in the Moonlight.* Surely no stranger moon shadow ever fell across the stanzas of an English poem than this huge and awful shadow of the Mariner's ship.

Why red? Did Coleridge recall, as Lowes suspects, reports of plankton that burned in the night with ruddy phosphorescence? Non-luminous "red seas" are even more common in the reports of voyagers. Charles Darwin, in his account of the voyage of *H.M.S. Beagle* (of course this was after Coleridge's time), describes a rusty sea off the coast of Chile. "The colour of the water, as seen at some distance, was like that of a river which has flowed through a red clay district; but under the shade of the vessel's side it was quite as dark as chocolate." In the sea near Tierra del Fuego, Darwin reports seeing narrow strips of a "bright red color," the color deriving from small crabs swarming on the surface. Floating seaweed can also impart a red color to the sea. While Coleridge was working on his ballad, Dorothy Wordsworth noted in her journal an occasion on which the sea was "gloomy red." In short, Coleridge had every reason to suppose that his red shadow was a possible sight. (For a discussion of the symbolic overtones of "red," see the section on Maud Bodkin in "Interpretations.")

When Thomas Love Peacock put Coleridge into his novel *Nightmare Abbey,* he called him Mr. Flosky, a corruption (as Peacock explains) of Filosky, from a Greek word meaning a lover of shadows. It is a perceptive description of Coleridge. *The Ancient Mariner* is a poem of light and shade. What is day and night except the state of being in and out of a shadow cast by the sun? What is sunrise and sunset except the retreating and advancing edge of that shadow? What is a crescent moon except a moon that is, for the most part, in shadow? The word "shadow" appears seven times in the ballad, eight if we include "shade," and still more if we count the "shadows" in lines that appear only in the ballad's first printing.

Coleridge was enamored of shadows in more than the literal sense; he was intoxicated by mystery,

In his loneliness and fixedness he yearneth towards the journeying Moon, and the stars that still sojourn, yet still move onward; and every where the blue sky belongs to them, and is their appointed rest, and their native country and their own natural homes, which they enter unannounced, as lords that are certainly expected and yet there is a silent joy at their arrival.

* The moving Moon went up the sky,
And no where did abide:
Softly she was going up,
And a star or two beside——**92**

Her beams bemocked the sultry main,**93**
Like April hoar-frost spread;
But where the ship's huge shadow lay,
270 The charmèd water burnt alway
A still and awful red.**94**

darkness, and the transcendental shadows of German metaphysics. As a Kantian, he saw the world itself as the shadow world of Plato's cave. "We cannot look directly into the nature of things," says Mr. Skioner in *Crotchet Castle* (Skioner is another of Peacock's several personifications of Coleridge); "we can only catch glimpses of the mighty shadow in the camera obscura of transcendental intelligence."

95. Water-snakes: It is impossible to say exactly what type of marine life is intended. The term "water-snake" was commonly used in Coleridge's day for any species of snake that frequented the water, especially in tropical regions. Such snakes are never far from land, however, whereas Coleridge's water-snakes are out on the wide sea. Lowes (Chap. III) marshals an abundance of quotations from the sea travel books which describe varicolored, luminescent snake-like forms that undoubtedly were the sources of Coleridge's water-snakes. These creatures probably belonged to a subdivision of the annelids (worms) called nemerteans (after Nemertes, a Greek sea nymph). They are beautifully colored, ribbon-like marine worms with lengths varying from less than an inch to more than 25 yards. Many of the species are luminescent.

96. Many commentators have called attention to the antiphony of this and the preceding stanza. *Outside* the ship's shadow the water-snakes shine in the moonlight with eerie whiteness; *inside* the ship's shadow their luminescent colors become visible.

97. In his poem "This Lime-tree Bower my Prison," written a few months before *The Ancient Mariner,* Coleridge describes an occasion on which he himself, his heart "awake to Love and Beauty," blesses a crow he sees flying through the twilight.

Note how the last two lines make it clear that the blessing of the snakes does not spring from the Mariner's own will; he is responding, unaware, to promptings from above. "This act of blessing does not *win* God's grace," writes R. L. Brett (*Reason and Imagination,* 1960); "it *is* God's grace."

98. So free: It is hard to say exactly what Coleridge intended by this phrase. Most commentators have taken it to mean "thus made free." The albatross is freed *as a result* of the Mariner's ability to pray. The word "so" is sometimes used, however, in the sense of "then" or "thereafter," in which case the phrase may mean nothing more than that the albatross was freed *after* the Mariner found himself able to pray.

It also is possible that "so" is intended to intensify the word "free," which in turn may modify either "albatross" or "neck." The Mariner may be saying: After I found I could pray, the albatross was so free that it dropped from my neck; or, from my neck, which suddenly felt extremely free, dropped the albatross.

99. Like lead: Coleridge is emphasizing the enormous weight of the burden that the Mariner feels has been lifted from his soul.

By the light of
the Moon he
beholdeth God's
creatures of the
great calm.

* Beyond the shadow of the ship,
I watched the water-snakes:**95**
They moved in tracks of shining white,
And when they reared, the elfish light
Fell off in hoary flakes.

Within the shadow of the ship**96**
I watched their rich attire:
Blue, glossy green, and velvet black,
280   They coiled and swam; and every track
Was a flash of golden fire.

Their beauty and
their happiness.

O happy living things! no tongue
Their beauty might declare:
A spring of love gushed from my heart,
And I blessed them unaware:

He blesseth them
in his heart.

Sure my kind saint took pity on me,
And I blessed them unaware.**97**

The spell begins
to break.

The self-same moment I could pray;
And from my neck so free**98**
290   The Albatross fell off, and sank
Like lead into the sea.**99**

PART V

100. Silly: "A remarkably happy word, as all readers must feel," remarks Kenneth Burke in his *Philosophy of Literary Form,* "and one certainly worthy of a gloss inquiring into its synecdochic functioning, its implications, its role as a representative of more than it explicitly says." For years, Burke writes, he thought about this word. "I noted the epithet as surprising, picturesque, and interesting. I knew that it was doing something, but I wasn't quite sure what." When Burke conceived of the pilot's boy as a scapegoat (see Note 166) he saw that "silly" was a "technical foreshadowing of the fate that befell this figure in the poem." In other words, as the buckets serve as vessels for the rain, so the crazed pilot's boy later serves as a vessel for the Mariner's punishment.

Perhaps. But this seems farfetched even on the assumption, itself dubious, that the pilot's boy *is* a scapegoat. At any rate, on a less subtle level the word "silly" certainly conveys a sense of absurdity; the buckets are ridiculous because they are useless. They "had so long remained" on deck, completely empty, that they had acquired a foolish, functionless appearance, like an old abandoned pump at a well long dry.

101. Blessèd: This can be taken in two ways—blessed as opposed to damned, and blessed as opposed to the misery of the Mariner's life-in-death.

102. Anear: Near.

103. Sere: The word is now used exclusively to mean dried up and withered, like dead leaves, but

Coleridge here employs it in an obsolete sense that applies specifically to cloth. Sere cloth is cloth that has been worn to shreds. "Our sails," wrote Captain Shelvocke, in the travel book from which Coleridge took the shooting of the albatross (See Note 25), ". . . were now grown so very thin and rotten."

104. Sheen: Bright, shining, resplendent. (Cf., line 56, where "sheen" is used, in its more customary way, as a noun.)

105. This stanza seems to describe an aurora, but the aurora is a phenomenon of the poles and could not be seen if the ship is still near the Equator. One possibility: While the Mariner slept, his ship may have been driven north far enough to see the *aurora borealis,* or south far enough to see the *aurora australis* (see Note 119). Or, Coleridge simply may have drawn on descriptions of the aurora, in various books that he read, for depicting a miraculous airglow in *tropical* skies.

The aurora is a luminescence of the upper atmosphere in regions surrounding the two magnetic poles. It is now known to be caused by charged particles that stream from the sun, especially during periods of intense sunspot turbulence. (How Coleridge would have delighted to know this; it ties in so appropriately with the role of his "bloody sun"!) Auroral lights at times resemble the folds of enormous glowing draperies that seem to wave in the wind. Lowes (Chap. XI, Sec. 4) excerpts from travel books descriptions of auroras that may have influenced Coleridge's

PART V

Oh sleep! it is a gentle thing,
Beloved from pole to pole!
To Mary Queen the praise be given!
She sent the gentle sleep from Heaven,
That slid into my soul.

*By the grace of
the holy Mother,
the ancient
Mariner is
refreshed 300
with rain.*

The silly buckets on the deck,**100**
That had so long remained,
I dreamt that they were filled with dew;
And when I awoke, it rained.

My lips were wet, my throat was cold,
My garments all were dank;
Sure I had drunken in my dreams,
And still my body drank.

I moved, and could not feel my limbs:
I was so light—almost
I thought that I had died in sleep,
And was a blessèd ghost.**101**

*He heareth
sounds and seeth 310
strange sights
and commotions
in the sky and
the element.*

And soon I heard a roaring wind:
It did not come anear;**102**
But with its sound it shook the sails,
That were so thin and sere.**103**

imagery in this stanza. One writer
says the lights "make a rustling
and crackling noise, like the wav-
ing of a large flag in a fresh gale
of wind." Another writes of "fires
of a thousand colors" that "light
up the sky." The hyphenated word
"fire-flags" is Coleridge's own happy
invention.

If you fix your attention on a
cloud moving past the moon, the
cloud appears to be motionless
while the moon glides behind it.
Similarly, if attention is fixed on
the waving luminous folds of an
aurora, an illusion of moving or

The upper air burst into life!
And a hundred fire-flags sheen,**104**
To and fro they were hurried about!
And to and fro, and in and out,
The wan stars danced between.**105**

"dancing" is given to the "wan stars" that glimmer faintly through the folds. In his "Dejection: An Ode," written a few years later, Coleridge refers to essentially the same illusion:

> O Lady! in this wan and heartless mood,
> To other thoughts by yonder throstle woo'd,
>   All this long eve, so balmy and serene,
>   Have I been gazing on the western sky,
>   And its peculiar tint of yellow green:
> And still I gaze—and with how blank an eye!
> And those thin clouds above, in flakes and bars,
> That give away their motion to the stars;
> Those stars, that glide behind them or between,
> Now sparkling, now bedimmed, but always seen:
> Yon crescent Moon, as fixed as if it grew
> In its own cloudless, starless lake of blue;
> I see them all so excellently fair,
> I see, not feel, how beautiful they are!

106. Sigh like sedge: Like wind blowing through sedge. Note that it is only the *sound* of the "roaring wind" that shakes the sails (see line 311). The wind itself, if true wind it be, is high in the "upper air" where it presumably ripples the fire-flags. Many of the travel books speak of sounds accompanying the aurora (see previous note). The "loud wind" never touches the ship, as we learn in line 327—but see also Note 108.

107. Jag: Tooth-like projection.

Lowes makes out a strong case (Chap. XI, Sec. 4) for William

Bartram's *Travels* as the source of Coleridge's cleft black cloud from which sheet lightning, with never a jagged bolt, pours like a river. Bartram writes of "continuous streams or rivers of lightning pouring from the clouds," of lightning that opened "a fiery chasm in the black cloud," and of a hurricane that "comes on roaring . . . the dark cloud opens over my head, developing a vast river of the etherial fire."

There is no need, however, to assume that sheet lightning is intended by the reference to a jagless river. A bolt of lightning never zig-zags, the way it does in cartoons. As any photograph of a lightning bolt reveals, it strongly resembles an aerial view of a twisting river.

In the Freudian game of searching for sex symbols in poems, nothing scores higher than finding a symbol of the "primal scene." David Beres, whose psychoanalytic study of *The Ancient Mariner* is discussed in "Interpretations," finds the primal scene in this stanza and the two that precede it. My own preferences: Part I, stanzas 11 and 12; Part II, stanzas 5 and 6; Part V, stanzas 1, 21, 22.

108. Like the spectre ship in Part III, the Mariner's ship now moves through the sea without the aid of wind. The word "inspired" in the gloss has the sense of "inspirited"; in fact, the word *is* "inspirited" in the first printing of the gloss in *Sibylline Leaves*. Note that in the original version of the ballad the first two lines of this stanza have the roaring wind dropping like a stone on both ship and water.

And the coming wind did roar more
    loud,
And the sails did sigh like sedge;**106**
* And the rain poured down from one
    black cloud;
The Moon was at its edge.

The thick black cloud was cleft, and still
The Moon was at its side:
Like waters shot from some high crag,
The lightning fell with never a jag,**107**
A river steep and wide.

The bodies of the
ship's crew are
inspired and the
ship moves on:

The loud wind never reached the ship,
Yet now the ship moved on!**108**
Beneath the lightning and the Moon
The dead men gave a groan.

They groaned, they stirred, they all up-
    rose,
* Nor spake, nor moved their eyes;
It had been strange, even in a dream,
To have seen those dead men rise.

320

330

109. 'Gan: Began. The contraction appears again in line 385.

110. Wont: Accustomed.

111. We have Wordsworth's word for it that it was he who suggested to Coleridge the ship be navigated by dead men. Whether Wordsworth thought of this himself or merely recalled a legend of the sea, we do not know. It is also possible that Coleridge, after the hint by Wordsworth, remembered one or more such legends. At any rate, stories of ships navigated by dead men were part of the sea's oral tradition, and could easily have reached the ears of either poet. A few are recounted in Lowes (Chap. XV, Sec. 4) and he gives references to others. O course legends of revenants (reanimated dead bodies) go back to ancient times; here we are concerned only with ships operated by revenants. Coleridge was the first to exploit such a theme in a literary masterpiece, and no one has done it better since.

Strictly speaking, the ship is not navigated by the dead men, but by a troop of angels who reanimate the bodies. Here, Coleridge was probably influenced by a fourth-century letter, written by Paulinus, Bishop of Nola. (That Coleridge borrowed from this letter was first suggested by an anonymous author in an article on "The Original Ancient Mariner," in *Gentleman's Magazine,* October, 1853.) Paulinus tells the story of a ship abandoned in a storm by everyone in the crew except an old man who had been below operating a pump. For six days the old man is alone on the ship, terrified, lonely, longing for death. The Lord takes pity on him, and sends an angelic band to operate the ship and steer it safely back to harbor. There are no reanimated bodies in this tale, but many of its details correspond with details in Coleridge's ballad. Most commentators agree that Coleridge probably saw an edition of Paulinus and that it gave him the idea of having angels take control of the ship.

112. Humphry House, in his *Coleridge,* comments on this stanza: "This brings home, as nothing else does, the horror of the deaths, the violation of family ties which the action has involved; it dramatizes to the Mariner's consciousness the utter ruin of the merry, unified community which had set out on the voyage. The curse in the stony eyes (lines 436–41) is made far more appalling by this specially intimate experience of the fact that intimacy was gone for ever."

113. Corses: Corpses.

114. The Mariner's guardian saint has been mentioned earlier in line 286. Coleridge's suggestion in the gloss that this saint is responsible for the sending down of the angels has, writes McElderry (in the article cited in Note 39) "all the appearance of an afterthought."

115. "The last syllable of 'jargoning' should not be stressed, but pronounced lightly as in prose," wrote William Vaughn Moody. "The effect of rhyme thus produced by an unstressed syllable matching one of heavy stress is very delicate and beautiful." For the possible influence of Chaucer on the choice of the word "jargoning," as well as other words in this stanza and the next, see Note 181 on the original version of the poem.

The helmsman steered, the ship moved
    on;
Yet never a breeze up-blew;
The mariners all 'gan work the ropes,**109**
Where they were wont to do;**110**
They raised their limbs like lifeless
    tools—
340 We were a ghastly crew.**111**

The body of my brother's son
Stood by me, knee to knee:
The body and I pulled at one rope,
But he said nought to me.**112**

But not by the
souls of the men,
nor by daemons
of earth or
middle air, but
by a blessed
troop of angelic
spirits, sent down
by the invocation 350
of the
guardian saint.**114**

"I fear thee, ancient Mariner!"
Be calm, thou Wedding-Guest!
'Twas not those souls that fled in pain,
Which to their corses came again,**113**
But a troop of spirits blest:

For when it dawned—they dropped their
    arms,
And clustered round the mast;
Sweet sounds rose slowly through their
    mouths,
And from their bodies passed.

Around, around, flew each sweet sound,
Then darted to the Sun;
Slowly the sounds came back again,
Now mixed, now one by one.

Sometimes a-dropping from the sky
I heard the sky-lark sing;
360 Sometimes all little birds that are,
How they seemed to fill the sea and air
With their sweet jargoning!**115**

116. The sound of the sails is not caused by a wind that is blowing the ship; we are told explicitly in the next two stanzas that the ship is moved from beneath by the polar water daemon. One presumes that the sails are curving toward the stern and shaking gently in the pseudo-breeze produced by the ship's forward motion through the still air. Note in line 381 that the noise of the sails ceases as soon as the ship is becalmed.

117. Fathom: Six feet.

118. Control of the ship has passed from the daemons to the angels of the Lord, even though the underwater daemon is still the agency that moves the ship. The daemon now moves the ship reluctantly.

119. The sun above the mast indicates, and Coleridge's gloss makes it explicit, that the ship has once more reached the Equator. Here arises a curious problem that has troubled many commentators. For all we are told, the ship was still at the Line when the reanimated bodies began to navigate it; yet after sailing for some time, it reaches the Line again!

On the assumption that this is not just carelessness on the poet's part, we must assume that the ship has drifted or has been carried a considerable distance away from the Equator since it first was becalmed. The fact that the steersman was at his post in line 207 suggests that the ship may have been drifting even then, and there was ample time for the ship to have been driven north or south, by natural or supernatural agencies, during the Mariner's long sleep at the beginning of Part V. That this occurred is implied by the Mariner's witnessing of a polar aurora in the sixth stanza of Part V.

Obviously there is a puzzle here, and unfortunately Coleridge left no record of what, if anything, he had in mind. That the ship had been carried north seems unlikely, because the daemon moving the ship lives at the South Pole and would scarcely be expected to operate in northern waters (see the following note). More likely, the polar spirit, seeking vengeance, drags the ship south while the Mariner sleeps, hoping to get the ship into antarctic waters. The Mariner awakes, and sees the *aurora australis*. The angelic troop takes command, and forces the daemon to return the ship to the Equator.

Here, again, there are two possibilities: (1) the ship had not been carried far south, and is returned to the Line in mid-Pacific, (2) the ship had been carried to polar waters off the Cape of Good Hope, and is returned to the Line in mid-Atlantic. (See Note 105.) The second alternative seems more likely in view of Coleridge's first marginal note to Part VI, which states that the ship is carried miraculously *northward* immediately after the polar daemon leaves. Since the ship is then homeward bound, it apparently has rounded the Cape of Good Hope; otherwise it would have to travel south to round the Cape. Also, rounding the Cape would carry the ship far enough south to make the appearance of the southern lights plausible.

120. Lane Cooper, in his article on "The Power of the Eye in Cole-

And now 'twas like all instruments,
Now like a lonely flute;
And now it is an angel's song,
That makes the heavens be mute.

* It ceased; yet still the sails made on
A pleasant noise till noon,**116**
A noise like of a hidden brook
In the leafy month of June,
That to the sleeping woods all night
Singeth a quiet tune.

Till noon we quietly sailed on,
Yet never a breeze did breathe:
Slowly and smoothly went the ship,
Moved onward from beneath.

Under the keel nine fathom deep,**117**
From the land of mist and snow,
The spirit slid: and it was he
That made the ship to go.**118**
The sails at noon left off their tune,
And the ship stood still also.

The Sun, right up above the mast,**119**
Had fixed her to the ocean:**120**
But in a minute she 'gan stir,
With a short uneasy motion—
Backwards and forwards half her length
With a short uneasy motion.**121**

370

The lonesome
Spirit from the
south-pole
carries on the
ship as far as the   380
Line, in
obedience to
the angelic troop,
but still requireth
vengeance.

ridge," thinks that this line implies that the sun exerts a magic power on the ship, something akin to the evil eye (see Note 8). In other words, the sun has becalmed the ship, making it impossible for the polar spirit to continue moving it. Lowes finds this suggestion plausible. It gains strength from the fact that, in the ballad's next Part, the moon serves as a guiding agency in moving the ship northward.

An alternative interpretation assumes that the ship has been carried north to the Equator and that the south polar daemon is not permitted to cross the Line. As soon as the ship reaches the Line it becomes

fixed to the spot. There is no need to suppose an actual force connecting sun and ship. The sun above the mast is merely a sign that the Equator has been reached and the daemon can go no farther.

121. "The extra syllable of the rhyme-lines, and the shifted accents in lines 3 and 5, suggest uneasiness. The repetition of line 4 suggests the monotonous back and fill of the ship." (William Vaughn Moody.)

122. The ship is convulsed when the water daemon, nine fathom deep, releases his hold on the ship. One imagines the daemon angrily moving the ship back and forth with a "short, uneasy motion" as he realizes he has reached the Line and must abandon his power over the ship. Frustrated in his vengeance, he gives the ship a last violent shake before he finally lets go and returns to the South Pole. He has, however, as the next marginal note makes clear, obtained from the higher powers—the Christian hierarchy of saints and angels—a promise that the Mariner "hath penance more to do."

It has been pointed out (by C. S. Wilkinson in his *Wake of the Bounty*) that in the line about the pawing horse suddenly leaping forward, Coleridge may have remem-

bered one of his own unhappy experiences on horseback when he was a member of the King's Regiment.

123. Have not: Am unable.

124. Living life: In contrast to his death-in-life, before his kind saint took pity on him.

125. By him who died on cross: A common medieval oath.

126. Honey-dew: A sweet, sticky substance that exudes from the leaves of certain trees and other plants in hot weather; it was thought at one time to have an origin like dew. More poetically, as used here, the term refers to a supernal substance, deliciously sweet, believed to fall from the heavens like manna. Coleridge mentions it again in "Kubla Khan"

For he on honey-dew hath fed
And drunk the milk of Paradise.

Then like a pawing horse let go,
390 She made a sudden bound:**122**
  * It flung the blood into my head,
And I fell down in a swound.

How long in that same fit I lay,
I have not to declare;**123**
But ere my living life returned,**124**
  * I heard and in my soul discerned
Two voices in the air.

The Polar Spirit's fellow-daemons, the invisible inhabitants of the element, take part in his wrong; and two of them relate, one to the other, that penance long and heavy for the ancient Mariner hath been accorded to the Polar Spirit, who returneth southward.

400

"Is it he?" quoth one, "Is this the man?
By him who died on cross,**125**
With his cruel bow he laid full low
The harmless Albatross.

The spirit who bideth by himself
In the land of mist and snow,
He loved the bird that loved the man
Who shot him with his bow."

The other was a softer voice,
As soft as honey-dew:**126**
Quoth he, "The man hath penance done,
And penance more will do."

85

PART VI

127. Blast: Wind.

128. The ocean, like a slave, looks up to the moon to find out what he is supposed to do. Critics have suggested that Coleridge's figure of speech was borrowed from the following lines in "Orchestra," a poem by John Davies:

> For his great chrystal eye is always cast
> Up to the moon, and on her fixed fast.

129. The moon is, of course, the cause of ocean tides. It is the ocean, not the moon, that is sometimes smooth, sometimes grim.

130. While the Mariner is in a trance, angelic powers speed the ship northward, the moon serving as a guide. If our plotting of the journey is correct (see Note 119), the ship had been carried around the Cape of Good Hope by the water daemon, and is now being transported north to its home harbor in Scotland or Northern England. As Lowes points out, Coleridge surely must have recalled the similarly miraculous episode in Homer's *Odyssey*, in which the gods cause a deep sleep to fall on Ulysses while his ship (as Poe describes it in "To Helen"):

> . . . gently, o'er a perfumed sea,
> The weary, way-worn wanderer bore
> To his own native shore.

The reference to the air being cut away in front and closing from behind is apparently an attempt to introduce a quasi-scientific explanation of the event. A vacuum forms in front of the ship, then pressure of the air in back moves the ship forward.

131. Belated: Made late.

PART VI

FIRST VOICE

410 "But tell me, tell me! speak again,
Thy soft response renewing—
What makes that ship drive on so fast?
What is the ocean doing?"

SECOND VOICE

"Still as a slave before his lord,
The ocean hath no blast; **127**
His great bright eye most silently
Up to the Moon is cast—**128**

If he may know which way to go;
For she guides him smooth or grim.**129**
420 See, brother, see! how graciously
She looketh down on him."

FIRST VOICE

The Mariner hath been cast into a trance; for the angelic power causeth the vessel to drive northward faster than human life could endure.

* "But why drives on that ship so fast,
Without or wave or wind?"

SECOND VOICE

"The air is cut away before,
And closes from behind.**130**

Fly, brother, fly! more high, more high!
Or we shall be belated:**131**
For slow and slow that ship will go,
When the Mariner's trance is abated."

87

132. The bodies were more fit for a charnel-dungeon (the place where bodies, in the Middle Ages, were put before burial) than the deck of a ship.

133. Ocean green: Green is traditionally used by English poets for describing the ocean, especially the ocean near the shore. Here the word carries the suggestion of a natural ocean in contrast to the "rotting sea" of earlier stanzas.

134. Else: The word is probably intended in an obsolete sense which the *Oxford English Dictionary* gives as "at another time" or "formerly." The Mariner is able now to turn his eyes from the dead men and look at the sea, but because of his fear he does not see (as he had seen before when the ship first sailed, perhaps many times before) the familiar sight of his home harbor in the distance.

The line, as it appears in the ballad's first version ("Of what might else be seen"), has a slightly different meaning. In this context "else" must be interpreted as "otherwise."

135. Opposite this stanza, in the margin of a copy of *Sibylline*

Leaves, is a penciled note (believed to have been written by one of Coleridge's younger disciples) that reads simply: "From Dante." On the basis of this hint, Lowes read through the *Divine Comedy* until he came to the following passage in the twenty-first canto of *The Inferno,* lines 25–30. Lowes quotes from John Aiken Carlyle's prose translation:

> Then I turned round, like one who longs to see what he must shun, and who is dashed with sudden fear, so that he puts not off his flight to look; and behind us I saw a black Demon come running up the cliff.

136. A breeze ripples the sea, but what is meant by "in shade" is not clear. Perhaps it refers to cloud shadows moving across the water as the clouds travel with the wind. Perhaps it means that wind-rippled water acquires a darker shade. The second interpretation is strengthened by entry 1589 in *The Notebooks of Samuel Taylor Coleridge,* Vol. I, Part I, which begins: "Images. Shadow of the Tree in the ruffled water distinguishable from the Breeze on the water only by its stationariness."

The supernatural **430**
motion is
retarded; the
Mariner awakes,
and his penance
begins anew.

I woke, and we were sailing on
As in a gentle weather:
'Twas night, calm night, the moon was
  high;
The dead men stood together.

All stood together on the deck,
For a charnel-dungeon fitter:**132**
All fixed on me their stony eyes,
That in the Moon did glitter.

The pang, the curse, with which they
  died,
Had never passed away:
440 I could not draw my eyes from theirs,
Nor turn them up to pray.

The curse is
finally expiated.

And now this spell was snapt: once
  more
I viewed the ocean green,**133**
And looked far forth, yet little saw
Of what had else been seen—**134**

Like one, that on a lonesome road
Doth walk in fear and dread,
And having once turned round walks on,
And turns no more his head;
450 Because he knows, a frightful fiend
Doth close behind him tread.**135**

But soon there breathed a wind on me,
Nor sound nor motion made:
Its path was not upon the sea,
In ripple or in shade.**136**

137. "We sailed softly west northwest," wrote one of the old mariners (Lowes, Chap. XVII, Sec. 3), but whether Coleridge borrowed the phrase or independently thought of it is anybody's guess.

138. As the ship returns to harbor, the Mariner sees the three objects —light-house, hill, church—in reverse order from which they were previously mentioned (lines 23–24) when the ship left the harbor.

139. Countree: An archaic spelling of "country," used often in old English ballads and their modern imitations.

140. Harbour-bar: The ridge of sand that forms across the mouth of harbors.

141. May this be a reality and not a dream, but if it *is* a dream, keep me dreaming. Similar phrases have often been uttered by Christian ecstatics, and are embodied in more than one Protestant hymn (*e.g.,* "Let me dream on, if I am dreaming. / Let me dream on, my sins are gone").

Alway: A poetic, archaic form of "always." The word has appeared earlier, in line 270.

142. Strewn: Calmed. The *Oxford English Dictionary* gives the following poetic use of the verb strew: "To level, calm (stormy waves); to allay (a storm)." So calm was the harbor that it had a glassy appearance.

143. The word "shadow" is sometimes synonymous with reflected image. The moon's reflection is visible in the water of the bay.

It raised my hair, it fanned my cheek
Like a meadow-gale of spring—
It mingled strangely with my fears,
Yet it felt like a welcoming.

460 Swiftly, swiftly flew the ship,
Yet she sailed softly too:**137**
Sweetly, sweetly blew the breeze—
On me alone it blew.

And the ancient
Mariner
beholdeth his
native country.

Oh! dream of joy! is this indeed
The light-house top I see?
Is this the hill? is this the kirk?**138**
Is this mine own countree?**139**

We drifted o'er the harbour-bar,**140**
And I with sobs did pray—
470 O let me be awake, my God!
Or let me sleep alway.**141**

The harbour-bay was clear as glass,
So smoothly it was strewn!**142**
* And on the bay the moonlight lay,
And the shadow of the Moon.**143**

144. Steady: Unmoved by any breeze.

145. The Mariner is standing at the edge of the deck, perhaps on the forecastle, looking forward toward the moonlit bay. The brightness of the hill and church suggests that the moon is behind the ship. In the water, a short distance from the prow (as we learn in the next stanza) he sees the "crimson shadows" of the seraphs before he turns his head to view them directly. The crimson symbolizes, perhaps, the albatross' blood (see line 513), and the blood of Christ by which he is cleansed of his sin.

Exactly what is meant by "crimson shadows"? Coleridge probably intended nothing more than crimson reflections in the water, without realizing that it is impossible to stand on a ship's deck and see in the sea a reflection of anything on deck. (Of course the reflections would be visible to someone *outside* the ship. Cf. Note 41 for a similar confusion of how things look to observers on and off a ship.) Most commentators have assumed the shadows to be reflections; apparently they too did not know that the Mariner could not see them.

One might argue that the crimson shadows actually *are* shadows.

The full moon behind the ship, shining through translucent crimson seraphs, could throw genuine red-tinged shadows on the water—shadows that *would* be visible to the Mariner. That Coleridge did not have this in mind is evident from stanzas which he removed from his original version. Before the seraph forms rise above the lifeless corpses, the animated bodies themselves, their right arms burning like torches, are seen reflected in the water as "dark-red shadows," while the Mariner's own flesh is red from the smoky glare of the torchlight.

146. Holy Rood: The cross on which Jesus was crucified. "By the Holy Rood" was a familiar medieval oath.

147. In Christian mythology the seraphim are the highest order of angels, excelling all others in the fervor of their love, as distinguished from the cherubim, the second highest order, who excel in knowledge. In medieval art the seraphim were traditionally given a red color. They have six wings and serve as guardians of God's throne (see Isaiah, Chap. 6). Milton, in *Paradise Lost*, is believed to have been the first to shorten the word to "seraph."

The angelic
spirits leave the
dead bodies,

And appear in
their own forms
of light.

The rock shone bright, the kirk no less,
That stands above the rock:
The moonlight steeped in silentness
The steady weathercock.**144**

480   And the bay was white with silent light,
Till rising from the same,
* Full many shapes, that shadows were,
In crimson colours came.**145**

A little distance from the prow
Those crimson shadows were:
I turned my eyes upon the deck—
Oh, Christ! what saw I there!

Each corse lay flat, lifeless and flat,
And, by the holy rood!**146**
490   A man all right, a seraph-man,**147**
On every corse there stood.

148. It was in response to these signals that the Pilot set out in his boat (see line 526). When a ship enters a large harbor, it is boarded by a harbor pilot who takes control of the ship to guide it efficiently into its assigned berth.

149. Impart: Make known, communicate. In other words, the seraphs said nothing.

150. Cheer: The Pilot's call to the ship.

151. Perforce: By the force of circumstances. Fascinated as he was by what he saw on deck, the sound of oars and the Pilot's voice compel him to turn his gaze back again toward the bay.

152. Blast: Destroy.

153. A boat approaches the ship, carrying the Pilot, his boy assistant, and a hermit. The Hermit, we learn in the next Part, lives a life of solitary contemplation in a wood near the harbor, where he prays by kneeling on a moss-covered stump. He is a type of ascetic common in the Middle Ages, and often encountered in medieval literature.

154. Shrieve: A variant spelling of "shrive." It means to hear someone's confession of sin, and to give absolution.

* This seraph-band, each waved his hand:
It was a heavenly sight!
They stood as signals to the land,**148**
Each one a lovely light;

This seraph-band, each waved his hand,
No voice did they impart—**149**
No voice; but oh! the silence sank
Like music on my heart.

500 But soon I heard the dash of oars,
I heard the Pilot's cheer;**150**
My head was turned perforce away**151**
And I saw a boat appear.

The Pilot and the Pilot's boy,
I heard them coming fast:
Dear Lord in Heaven! it was a joy
The dead men could not blast.**152**

I saw a third—I heard his voice:
It is the Hermit good!**153**
510 He singeth loud his godly hymns
That he makes in the wood.
He'll shrieve my soul, he'll wash away**154**
The Albatross's blood.

PART VII

155. Rears: Raises.

156. I trow: I suppose, or I do believe.

157. "That" is the subject of "made": the lights that have just made a signal.

158. Cf. line 120.

159. Ivy-tod: Ivy bush.

160. The owl, in England, is traditionally associated with the ivy bush; the bush's dense foliage furnishes a convenient spot where the bird can hide by day. A proverbial phrase, "He looks like an owl in an ivy bush," applies to anyone who appears particularly owlish; for example, a judge wearing his wig and a solemn, vacant expression.

It was widely believed in Coleridge's day that the male wolf, in periods of extreme hunger, killed and devoured its own children. Modern authorities on wild animals regard this as unfounded folklore, along with many other old wives' tales that exaggerate the wolf's rapaciousness. The ship's fiendish appearance seems to call to the Hermit's mind this supposed fiendish behavior of the wolf; perhaps Coleridge is reminding us that love for all things small and great is hardly characteristic of nature in the raw.

PART VII

This Hermit good lives in that wood
Which slopes down to the sea.
How loudly his sweet voice he rears!**155**
He loves to talk with marineres
That come from a far countree.

He kneels at morn, and noon, and eve—
He hath a cushion plump:
It is the moss that wholly hides
The rotted old oak-stump.

The skiff-boat neared: I heard them talk,
"Why, this is strange, I trow!**156**
Where are those lights so many and fair,
That signal made but now?"**157**

"Strange, by my faith!" the Hermit
    said—
"And they answered not our cheer!
The planks looked warped!**158** and see those
    sails,
How thin they are and sere!
I never saw aught like to them,
Unless perchance it were

Brown skeletons of leaves that lag
My forest-brook along;
When the ivy-tod is heavy with snow,**159**
And the owlet whoops to the wolf below,
That eats the she-wolf's young."**160**

97

161. The poem does not reveal who is responsible for the monstrous sound that shakes sea and sky, and sinks the Mariner's ship like lead. Some commentators have conjectured that the polar spirit destroys the ship in a last outburst of anger, but this seems unlikely because we are told in the gloss to Part V that the daemon "returneth southward." More likely, the ship was sunk by the angelic forces. Lowes thinks Coleridge may have been influenced by the Ulysses episode in Dante's *Inferno,* in which Ulysses tells how his ship went down in antarctic waters; but the connection seems tenuous.

162. After a week or more, drowned bodies rise to the surface.

163. This has been taken to imply that the dreadful sound flings the Mariner's floating body into the Pilot's boat, but the gloss suggests otherwise. The Mariner, rescued by the Pilot and his associates, is in such a stunned state that his rescue seems to him like a swift dream.

164. Telling of the sound: Echoing the sound.

"Dear Lord! it hath a fiendish look—
(The Pilot made reply)
540 I am a-feared"—"Push on, push on!"
Said the Hermit cheerily.

The boat came closer to the ship,
But I nor spake nor stirred;
The boat came close beneath the ship,
And straight a sound was heard.

The ship
suddenly sinketh.

Under the water it rumbled on,
* Still louder and more dread:
It reached the ship, it split the bay;
The ship went down like lead.**161**

The ancient
Mariner is   550
saved in the
Pilot's boat.

Stunned by that loud and dreadful
     sound,
Which sky and ocean smote,
Like one that hath been seven days
     drowned
My body lay afloat;**162**
But swift as dreams, myself I found
Within's the Pilot's boat.**163**

* Upon the whirl, where sank the ship,
The boat spun round and round;
And all was still, save that the hill
Was telling of the sound.**164**

165. The Pilot shrieks because he had assumed the Mariner to be dead. The silent motion of the Mariner's lips is more frightful than speech. Note (line 543) that the Mariner had neither moved nor spoken as the boat approached the ship.

166. Kenneth Burke, in *Philosophy of Literary Form,* argues that the presence of the Pilot's boy in the poem "cannot be understood at all, except in superficial terms of the interesting or the picturesque, if we do not grasp his function as a scapegoat of some sort—a victimized vessel for drawing off the most malign aspects of the curse that afflicts the 'greybeard loon' whose cure has been effected under the dubious aegis of moonlight."

A shaky conjecture. The unearthly noise, the sudden sinking of the ship, the spinning round and round of the Pilot's boat, and the apparent reanimation of a drowned body, seem sufficient to unhinge a boy's mind. The event is more than just "interesting or picturesque." Like the Pilot's fit, it dramatizes the scene's terror, accentuates the holy calm of the Hermit. There is nothing to suggest that the boy is more than temporarily crazed by the events witnessed; in fact, the Pilot himself, who fell down in a fit, makes as good a scapegoat as the boy.

167. Crossed his brow: Made the sign of the cross on his forehead, to protect himself against evil.

168. The Hermit, before he grants forgiveness, wants to know if the Mariner is really a man, and not a drowned body reanimated by a daemon, or, as the Pilot's boy suggests, by the Devil himself.

560 * I moved my lips—the Pilot shrieked**165**
    And fell down in a fit;
    The holy Hermit raised his eyes,
    And prayed where he did sit.

    I took the oars: the Pilot's boy,
    Who now doth crazy go,**166**
    Laughed loud and long, and all the
      while
    His eyes went to and fro.
    "Ha! ha!" quoth he, "full plain I see,
    The Devil knows how to row."

570 And now, all in my own countree,
    I stood on the firm land!
    The Hermit stepped forth from the boat,
    And scarcely he could stand.

The ancient
Mariner earnestly
entreateth the
Hermit to shrieve
him; and the
penance of Life
falls on him.

 * "O shrieve me, shrieve me, holy man!"
    The Hermit crossed his brow.**167**
    "Say quick," quoth he, "I bid thee say—
    What manner of man art thou?"**168**

    Forthwith this frame of mine was
      wrenched
    With a woful agony,
580 Which forced me to begin my tale;
    And then it left me free.

169. Night is a shadow that sweeps continually, swiftly, silently around the entire earth.

170. Part of the Mariner's penance is to wander from land to land, periodically wrenched with agony until he finds a man to whom he can tell his ghastly tale. The occult power of the old seaman's eye, his strange power of speech, make it impossible for the listener to break away until the tale has been told.

In Chapter XIV, entitled "How an Old Navigator Met Strange Company in Limbo," Lowes offers convincing evidence that Coleridge was strongly influenced here by two great legends of Christianity: the Wandering Jew and the wandering of Cain.

The legend of the Wandering Jew had its origin in John 21:22. The risen Christ is walking with his disciples. Peter sees John following them and asks, "What shall this man do?" Christ replies, "If I will that he tarry till I come, what is that to thee?" The disciples took this to mean that John would not die before the Second Coming, but John hastens to add that Jesus did not tell him that he would not die, but only that *"If* I will that he tarry . . ." In other words, the statement was not a prediction about John; but it did imply that Christ possessed the power to prevent a man from dying until he returned.

On another occasion Christ declared: "Verily I say unto you, There be some standing here, which shall not taste of death, till they see the Son of man coming in his kingdom." (Matthew 16:28. See also Mark 9:1 and Luke 9:27.)

Upon these two enigmatic re-marks of Jesus, the legend of the Wandering Jew arose: a man condemned to roam the earth, unable to die until Christ returns. The development of such a legend was almost inevitable, considering the circumstances. Taken at face value, Christ's words about his Second Coming imply that the event will take place within the lifetime of someone present. After a few centuries had gone by, this interpretation could no longer be given to his statement. Yet it was unthinkable that Christ could have uttered an untruth. The simplest way out: the Wandering Jew.

In some versions of the legend, the wanderer is a doorkeeper in the judgment hall of Pilate. In other versions he is a cobbler at whose door Jesus had paused when he was carrying his cross, and who angrily pushed Jesus away. Hundreds of novels, poems, and plays about the Wandering Jew have been written. Lowes cites those most likely to have come to Coleridge's attention. From time to time, until as late as the nineteenth century, imposters and psychotics have turned up claiming to be the Wandering Jew, and many pious and sincere believers have been taken in. A reader interested in the idiotic details of this dreary history should consult *Curious Myths of the Middle Ages*, by Sabine Baring-Gould, the English writer who wrote the words of "Onward Christian Soldiers."

Cain, as we learn in Chapter 4 of Genesis, likewise was condemned to be a wanderer, and for the crime of murder which may be symbolized by the Mariner's killing of the albatross. Cain's punishment also

Since then, at an uncertain hour,
That agony returns:
And till my ghastly tale is told,
This heart within me burns.

* I pass, like night, from land to land; **169**
I have strange power of speech;
* That moment that his face I see,
I know the man that must hear me:
To him my tale I teach. **170**

figures in many literary works, including a three-canto prose-poem called "The Wanderings of Cain" that Coleridge himself once hoped to write in collaboration with Wordsworth. According to their plan, Wordsworth was to write the first canto, Coleridge the second, and whoever finished his part first would write the third! In a prefatory note to his second canto, Coleridge gave an amusing account of what happened:

590

"Methinks I see his [Wordsworth's] grand and noble countenance as at the moment when having despatched my own portion of the task at full finger-speed, I hastened to him with my manuscript—that look of humorous despondency fixed on his almost blank sheet of paper, and then its silent mock-piteous admission of failure struggling with the sense of the exceeding ridiculousness of the whole

scheme—which broke up in a laugh: and the *Ancient Mariner* was written instead."

That the Wandering Jew was also much in Coleridge's mind is evident from many facts cited by Lowes. J. B. Beer, in his book *Coleridge the Visionary* (Chap. 5, Note 40), quotes a newly discovered fragment of Coleridge's conversation which fully confirms Lowes's opinion: "It is an enormous blunder . . . to represent the Ancient Mariner as an old man on board ship. He was in my mind the everlasting Wandering Jew—had told this story ten thousand times since the voyage, which was in his early youth and 50 years before."

171. Vesper bell: A bell announcing the evening prayer service.

172. Kenneth Burke, in *Philosophy of Literary Form,* several times refers to this passage as reflecting Coleridge's marital troubles: ". . . an explicit statement of preference for church, prayer, and companionship over marriage . . ." No one can deny that Coleridge's marriage, at the time he wrote *The Ancient Mariner,* was not a happy one, but to read this into the stanza seems to be stretching things. It is surely understandable that a lonely old man, deeply religious and penitent for his sins, would find a quiet church service sweeter than a noisy, uproarious marriage feast. Besides, young Coleridge's soon-to-develop passion for Sarah Hutchinson scarcely indicates that, at the time he wrote his ballad, he would have found vesper prayer services sweeter than thoughts of love for a woman.

* What loud uproar bursts from that door!
  The wedding-guests are there:
  But in the garden-bower the bride
  And bride-maids singing are:
  And hark the little vesper bell,**171**
  Which biddeth me to prayer!

  O Wedding-Guest! this soul hath been
  Alone on a wide wide sea;
* So lonely 'twas, that God himself
  Scarce seeméd there to be.

  O sweeter than the marriage-feast,
  'Tis sweeter far to me,
  To walk together to the kirk
  With a goodly company!—**172**

  To walk together to the kirk,
  And all together pray,
  While each to his great Father bends,
  Old men, and babes, and loving friends
  And youths and maidens gay!

600

And to teach, by his own example, love and reverence to all things that God made and loveth.

610
Farewell, farewell! but this I tell
To thee, thou Wedding-Guest!
He prayeth well, who loveth well
Both man and bird and beast.

He prayeth best, who loveth best
All things both great and small;
For the dear God who loveth us,
He made and loveth all.**173**

* The Mariner, whose eye is bright,
Whose beard with age is hoar,
620 Is gone: and now the Wedding-Guest
Turned from the bridegroom's door.**174**

He went like one that hath been stunned,
And is of sense forlorn:**175**
A sadder and a wiser man,
He rose the morrow morn.

173. Note how the four-fold repetition of "loveth," in this and the previous stanza, underlines the pivotal word of the moral.
174. The Wedding-Guest is too shattered by the Mariner's story to take part in the festivities.
175. Forlorn: Deprived.

PART III

The Rime of the Ancyent Marinere

as first printed in *Lyrical Ballads*, 1798

"By thy long grey beard and glittering eye,
Now wherefore stopp'st thou me?"

THE RIME OF THE ANCYENT
MARINERE

IN SEVEN PARTS

ARGUMENT

How a Ship having passed the Line was driven by Storms to
the cold Country towards the South Pole; and how from thence
she made her course to the Tropical Latitude of the Great Pacific
Ocean; and of the strange things that befell; and in what manner
the Ancyent Marinere came back to his own Country.

I

IT is an ancyent Marinere,
  And he stoppeth one of three:
"By thy long grey beard and thy glittering eye
  "Now wherefore stoppest me?

"The Bridegroom's doors are open'd wide,
  "And I am next of kin;
"The Guests are met, the Feast is set,—
  "May'st hear the merry din."

But still he holds the wedding-guest—
  There was a Ship, quoth he—   10
"Nay, if thou'st got a laughsome tale,
  "Marinere! come with me."

He holds him with his skinny hand,
  Quoth he, there was a Ship—
"Now get thee hence, thou grey-beard Loon!
  "Or my Staff shall make thee skip."

He holds him with his glittering eye—
  The wedding-guest stood still
And listens like a three year's child;
  The Marinere hath his will.   20

The Wedding-Guest sat on a stone:

He can not chuse but hear.

The Rime of the Ancyent Marinere in *Lyrical Ballads*, 1798

The wedding-guest sate on a stone,
　He cannot chuse but hear:
And thus spake on that ancyent man,
　The bright-eyed Marinere.

The Ship was cheer'd, the Harbour clear'd—
　Merrily did we drop
Below the Kirk, below the Hill,
　Below the Light-house top.

The Sun came up upon the left,
　Out of the Sea came he:　　　　　　　　　　30
And he shone bright, and on the right
　Went down into the Sea.

Higher and higher every day,
　Till over the mast at noon—
The wedding-guest here beat his breast,
　For he heard the loud bassoon.

The Bride hath pac'd into the Hall,
　Red as a rose is she;
Nodding their heads before her goes
　The merry Minstralsy.　　　　　　　　　　40

The wedding-guest he beat his breast,
　Yet he cannot chuse but hear:
And thus spake on that ancyent Man,
　The bright-eyed Marinere.

Listen, Stranger! Storm and Wind,
　A Wind and Tempest strong!
For days and weeks it play'd us freaks—
　Like Chaff we drove along.

Listen, Stranger! Mist and Snow,
　And it grew wond'rous cauld:　　　　　　　50
And Ice mast-high came floating by
　As green as Emerauld.

And thro' the drifts the snowy clifts
　Did send a dismal sheen;
Ne shapes of men ne beasts we ken—
　The Ice was all between.

111

The bride hath paced into the hall,
Red as a rose is she.

The ship drove fast, loud roared the blast,
And southward aye we fled.

And now there came both mist and snow,
And it grew wondrous cold.

The ice was here, the ice was there,
The ice was all around.

It ate the food it ne'er had eat.

. . . . With my cross-bow
I shot the Albatross.

The Ice was here, the Ice was there,
  The Ice was all around:
It crack'd and growl'd, and roar'd and howl'd—
  Like noises of a swound.   60

At length did cross an Albatross,
  Thorough the Fog it came;
And an it were a Christian Soul,
  We hail'd it in God's name.

The Marineres gave it biscuit-worms,**176**
  And round and round it flew:
The Ice did split with a Thunder-fit,
  The Helmsman steer'd us thro'.

And a good south wind sprung up behind,
  The Albatross did follow;   70
And every day for food or play
  Came to the Marinere's hollo!

In mist or cloud on mast or shroud,
  It perch'd for vespers nine,
Whiles all the night thro' fog-smoke white,
  Glimmer'd the white moon-shine.

"God save thee, ancyent Marinere!
  "From the fiends that plague thee thus—
·"Why look'st thou so?"—with my cross-bow
  I shot the Albatross.   80

176. See Part I, Note 27 of the
previous text.

II

The Sun came up upon the right,
　　Out of the Sea came he;
And broad as a weft upon the left**177**
　　Went down into the Sea.

And the good south wind still blew behind,
　　But no sweet Bird did follow
Ne any day for food or play
　　Came to the Marinere's hollo!

And I had done an hellish thing
　　And it would work 'em woe:　　　　　　　　90
For all averr'd, I had kill'd the Bird
　　That made the Breeze to blow.

Ne dim ne red, like God's own head,
　　The glorious Sun uprist:
Then all averr'd, I had kill'd the Bird
　　That brought the fog and mist.
'Twas right, said they, such birds to slay
　　That bring the fog and mist.

The breezes blew, the white foam flew,
　　The furrow follow'd free:　　　　　　　　100
We were the first that ever burst
　　Into that silent Sea.

177. Weft: A seafaring term with many alternate spellings (waffe, weffe, waif, waift, whiff, whift, wheft, waft, etc.). Originally it meant any sort of cloth that was used on a ship for giving a signal. Among sailors in Coleridge's time the word had a more specific meaning. It referred to a flag, rolled up into one long cylinder, tied to prevent it from unrolling, then hoisted to the top of the mast as a signal—usually a signal of distress. Coleridge had encountered the word in many travel books. Lowes cites numerous instances of its use, including one from Defoe's *Robinson Crusoe:* "We heard the ship fire a gun, and saw her make a waft with her ancient, as a signal for the boat to come on board."

Coleridge probably took the word out of his ballad because a contemporary reviewer (the same man who objected to "noises in a swound," see Note 24 of the poem's final version) spoke of the word as "nonsensical." Although a familiar term among sailors, it was not a literary word landsmen would understand.

And I had done a hellish thing,
And it would work 'em woe.

Down dropt the breeze, the Sails dropt down,
    'Twas sad as sad could be
And we did speak only to break
    The silence of the Sea.

All in a hot and copper sky
    The bloody sun at noon,
Right up above the mast did stand,
    No bigger than the moon.   110

Day after day, day after day,
    We stuck, ne breath ne motion,
As idle as a painted Ship
    Upon a painted Ocean.

Water, water, every where,
    And all the boards did shrink;
Water, water, every where,
    Ne any drop to drink.

The very deeps did rot: O Christ!
    That ever this should be!   120
Yea, slimy things did crawl with legs
    Upon the slimy Sea.

About, about, in reel and rout,
    The Death-fires danc'd at night;
The water, like a witch's oils,
    Burnt green and blue and white.

And some in dreams assured were
    Of the Spirit that plagued us so:
Nine fathom deep he had follow'd us
    From the Land of Mist and Snow.   130

And every tongue thro' utter drouth
    Was wither'd at the root;
We could not speak no more than if
    We had been choked with soot.

Ah wel-a-day! what evil looks
    Had I from old and young;
Instead of the Cross the Albatross
    About my neck was hung.

Water, water, every where,
Nor any drop to drink.

About, about, in reel and rout,
The death-fires danced at night.

Nine fathom deep he had followed us
From the land of mist and snow.

III

I saw a something in the Sky
   No bigger than my fist;
At first it seem'd a little speck
   And then it seem'd a mist:
It mov'd and mov'd, and took at last
   A certain shape, I wist.

A speck, a mist, a shape, I wist!
   And still it ner'd and ner'd;
And, an it dodg'd a water-sprite,
   It plung'd and tack'd and veer'd.

With throat unslack'd, with black lips bak'd
   Ne could we laugh, ne wail:
Then while thro' drouth all dumb they stood
I bit my arm and suck'd the blood
   And cry'd, A sail! a sail!

With throat unslack'd, with black lips bak'd
   Agape they hear'd me call:
Gramercy! they for joy did grin
And all at once their breath drew in
   As they were drinking all.

She doth not tack from side to side—
   Hither to work us weal
Withouten wind, withouten tide
   She steddies with upright keel.

The western wave was all a flame,
   The day was well nigh done!
Almost upon the western wave
   Rested the broad bright Sun;
When that strange shape drove suddenly
   Betwixt us and the Sun.

And strait the Sun was fleck'd with bars
   (Heaven's mother send us grace)
As if thro' a dungeon grate he peer'd
   With broad and burning face.

Alas! (thought I, and my heart beat loud)
   How fast she neres and neres!
Are these *her* Sails that glance in the Sun
   Like restless gossameres?

140

150

160

170

A speck, a mist, a shape, I wist!
And still it neared and neared.

Are those *her* naked ribs, which fleck'd
   The sun that did behind them peer?
And are these two all, all the crew,
   That woman and her fleshless Pheere?**178**   180

His bones were black with many a crack,
   All black and bare, I ween;
Jet-black and bare, save where with rust
Of mouldy damps and charnel crust
   They're patch'd with purple and green.

Her lips are red, *her* looks are free,
   Her locks are yellow as gold:
Her skin is as white as leprosy,
And she is far liker Death than he;
   Her flesh makes the still air cold.   190

The naked Hulk alongside came
   And the Twain were playing dice;
"The Game is done! I've won, I've won!"
   Quoth she, and whistled thrice.

A gust of wind sterte up behind
   And whistled thro' his bones;
Thro' the holes of his eyes and the hole of his mouth
   Half-whistles and half-groans.**179**

178. Pheere: Mate, spouse. The word was more commonly spelled "fere." (See Lowes's *The Road to Xanadu,* Chap. XVII, Note 106.)

179. Coleridge's decision to remove this stanza from the ballad (see Note 75 of the previous text) went unheeded by the printer of the first edition of *Sibylline Leaves,* but Coleridge was able to indicate its removal in the first entry on his errata page. Lowes quotes an amusing comment on this which Coleridge penned in the margin of a copy of the book: "This stanza I had earnestly charged the Printer to omit, but he was a coxcomb, and had an opinion of his own, forsooth! the Devil daub him! (i.e., his own devil)."

In another copy of the same edition he wrote (I quote again from Lowes): "This stanza was struck out by the Author, and reprinted either by the Oversight or the Self-opinion of the Printer, to whom the Author was indebted for various *intended* improvements of his Poems." Lowes adds: "And there are other pungent comments."

"The game is done! I've won, I've won!"
Quoth she, and whistles thrice.

Each turned his face with a ghastly pang,
And cursed me with his eye.

With never a whisper in the Sea
  Off darts the Spectre-ship;   200
While clombe above the Eastern bar
The horned Moon, with one bright Star
  Almost atween the tips.

One after one by the horned Moon
  (Listen, O Stranger! to me)
Each turn'd his face with a ghastly pang
  And curs'd me with his ee.

Four times fifty living men,
  With never a sigh or groan,
With heavy thump, a lifeless lump   210
  They dropp'd down one by one.

Their souls did from their bodies fly,—
  They fled to bliss or woe;
And every soul it pass'd me by,
  Like the whiz of my Cross-bow.

IV

"I fear thee, ancyent Marinere!
  "I fear thy skinny hand;
"And thou art long, and lank, and brown,
  "As is the ribb'd Sea-sand.

"I fear thee and thy glittering eye   220
  "And thy skinny hand so brown—"
Fear not, fear not, thou wedding-guest!
  This body dropt not down.

Alone, alone, all all alone
  Alone on the wide wide Sea;
And Christ would take no pity on
  My soul in agony.

The many men so beautiful,
  And they all dead did lie!
And a million million slimy things   230
  Liv'd on—and so did I.

I look'd upon the rotting Sea,
  And drew my eyes away;
I look'd upon the eldritch deck,**180**
  And there the dead men lay.

I look'd to Heav'n, and try'd to pray;
  But or ever a prayer had gusht,
A wicked whisper came and made
  My heart as dry as dust.

I clos'd my lids and kept them close,   240
  Till the balls like pulses beat;
For the sky and the sea, and the sea and the sky
Lay like a load on my weary eye,
  And the dead were at my feet.

180. Eldritch: Weird, frightful, hideous. ("Pearl . . .," writes Hawthorne in *The Scarlet Letter*, "gave an eldritch scream.")

And never a saint took pity on
My soul in agony.

I looked upon the rotting sea,
And drew my eyes away.

The cold sweat melted from their limbs,
  Ne rot, ne reek did they;
The look with which they look'd on me,
  Had never pass'd away.

An orphan's curse would drag to Hell
  A spirit from on high: 250
But O! more horrible than that
  Is the curse in a dead man's eye!
Seven days, seven nights I saw that curse,
  And yet I could not die.

The moving Moon went up the sky,
  And no where did abide:
Softly she was going up
  And a star or two beside—

Her beams bemock'd the sultry main
  Like morning frosts yspread;   260
But where the ship's huge shadow lay,
The charmed water burnt alway
  A still and awful red.

Beyond the shadow of the ship
  I watch'd the water-snakes:
They mov'd in tracks of shining white;
And when they rear'd, the elfish light
  Fell off in hoary flakes.

Within the shadow of the ship
  I watch'd their rich attire: 270
Blue, glossy green, and velvet black
They coil'd and swam; and every track
  Was a flash of golden fire.

O happy living things! no tongue
  Their beauty might declare:
A spring of love gusht from my heart,
  And I bless'd them unaware!
Sure my kind saint took pity on me,
  And I bless'd them unaware.

The self-same moment I could pray;   280
  And from my neck so free
The Albatross fell off, and sank
  Like lead into the sea.

Seven days, seven nights, I saw that curse,
And yet I could not die.

The moving Moon went up the sky.

Beyond the shadow of the ship,
I watched the water-snakes.

V

O sleep, it is a gentle thing,
  Belov'd from pole to pole!
To Mary-queen the praise be yeven
She sent the gentle sleep from heaven
  That slid into my soul.

The silly buckets on the deck
  That had so long remain'd,   290
I dreamt that they were fill'd with dew
  And when I awoke it rain'd.

My lips were wet, my throat was cold,
  My garments all were dank;
Sure I had drunken in my dreams
  And still my body drank.

I mov'd and could not feel my limbs,
  I was so light, almost
I thought that I had died in sleep,
  And was a blessed Ghost.   300

The roaring wind! it roar'd far off,
  It did not come anear;
But with its sound it shook the sails
  That were so thin and sere.

The upper air bursts into life,
  And a hundred fire-flags sheen
To and fro they are hurried about;
And to and fro, and in and out
  The stars dance on between.

The coming wind doth roar more loud;   310
  The sails do sigh, like sedge:
The rain pours down from one black cloud
  And the Moon is at its edge.

Hark! hark! the thick black cloud is cleft,
  And the Moon is at its side:
Like waters shot from some high crag,
The lightning falls with never a jag
  A river steep and wide.

The strong wind reach'd the ship: it roar'd
  And dropp'd down, like a stone!   320
Beneath the lightning and the moon
  The dead men gave a groan.

And the rain poured down from one black cloud.

They groan'd, they stirr'd, they all uprose,
    Ne spake, ne mov'd their eyes:
It had been strange, even in a dream
    To have seen those dead men rise.

The helmsman steer'd, the ship mov'd on;
    Yet never a breeze up-blew;
The Marineres all 'gan work the ropes,
    Where they were wont to do: 330
They rais'd their limbs like lifeless tools—
    We were a ghastly crew.

The body of my brother's son
    Stood by me knee to knee:
The body and I pull'd at one rope,
    But he said nought to me—
And I quak'd to think of my own voice
    How frightful it would be!

The day-light dawn'd—they dropp'd their arms,
    And cluster'd round the mast: 340
Sweet sounds rose slowly thro' their mouths
    And from their bodies pass'd.

Around, around, flew each sweet sound,
    Then darted to the sun:
Slowly the sounds came back again
    Now mix'd, now one by one.

Sometimes a dropping from the sky
    I heard the Lavrock sing;**181**
Sometimes all little birds that are
How they seem'd to fill the sea and air   350
    With their sweet jargoning.

181. Lavrock: Scottish word for lark. As Lowes points out (Chap. XVII, Sec. 4), both this word and "jargoning" in the last line were probably taken from the following lines in Chaucer's "Romaunt of the Rose":

There mightin men se many flockes
Of Turtels and of Laverockes . . .
Thei song ther song, as faire and wel
As angels doen espirituell . . .
Layis of love full wel souning
Thei songin in ther jargoning .

They groaned, they stirred, they all uprose,
Nor spake, nor moved their eyes.

It ceased; yet still the sails made on
A pleasant noise till noon.

And now 'twas like all instruments,
  Now like a lonely flute;
And now it is an angel's song
  That makes the heavens be mute.

It ceas'd: yet still the sails made on
  A pleasant noise till noon,
A noise like of a hidden brook
  In the leafy month of June,
That to the sleeping woods all night   360
  Singeth a quiet tune.

Listen, O listen, thou Wedding-guest!
  "Marinere! thou hast thy will:
"For that, which comes out of thine eye, doth make
  "My body and soul to be still."

Never sadder tale was told
  To a man of woman born:
Sadder and wiser thou wedding-guest!
  Thou'lt rise to-morrow morn.

Never sadder tale was heard   370
  By a man of woman born:
The Marineres all return'd to work
  As silent as beforne.

The Marineres all 'gan pull the ropes,
  But look at me they n'old: **182**
Thought I, I am as thin as air—
  They cannot me behold.

Till noon we silently sail'd on
  Yet never a breeze did breathe:
Slowly and smoothly went the ship   380
  Mov'd onward from beneath.

Under the keel nine fathom deep
  From the land of mist and snow
The spirit slid: and it was He
  That made the Ship to go.
The sails at noon left off their tune
  And the Ship stood still also.

182. N'old: Would not.

143

It flung the blood into my head,
And I fell down in a swound.

I heard, and in my soul discerned
Two voices in the air.

The sun right up above the mast
  Had fix'd her to the ocean:
But in a minute she 'gan stir   390
  With a short uneasy motion—
Backwards and forwards half her length
  With a short uneasy motion.

Then, like a pawing horse let go,
  She made a sudden bound:
It flung the blood into my head,
  And I fell into a swound.**183**

How long in that same fit I lay,
  I have not to declare;
But ere my living life return'd,   400
I heard and in my soul discern'd
  Two voices in the air,

"Is it he?" quoth one, "Is this the man?
  "By him who died on cross,
"With his cruel bow he lay'd full low
  "The harmless Albatross.

"The spirit who 'bideth by himself
  "In the land of mist and snow,
"He lov'd the bird that lov'd the man
  "Who shot him with his bow."   410

The other was a softer voice,
  As soft as honey-dew:
Quoth he "The man hath penance done,
  "And penance more will do."

183. Swound: Swoon. (See Note 24
of previous text.)

VI

First Voice

"But tell me, tell me! speak again,
  "Thy soft response renewing—
"What makes that ship drive on so fast?
  "What is the Ocean doing?"

Second Voice

"Still as a Slave before his Lord,
  "The Ocean hath no blast: 420
"His great bright eye most silently
  "Up to the moon is cast—

"If he may know which way to go,
  "For she guides him smooth or grim.
"See, brother, see! how graciously
  "She looketh down on him."

First Voice

"But why drives on that ship so fast
  "Withouten wave or wind?"

Second Voice

"The air is cut away before,
  "And closes from behind."   430

"Fly, brother, fly! more high, more high,
  "Or we shall be belated:
"For slow and slow that ship will go,
  "When the Marinere's trance is abated."

I woke, and we were sailing on
  As in a gentle weather:
'Twas night, calm night, the moon was high;
  The dead men stood together.

All stood together on the deck,
  For a charnel-dungeon fitter: 440
All fix'd on me their stony eyes
  That in the moon did glitter.

But why drives on that ship so fast,
Without or wave or wind?

The pang, the curse, with which they died,
  Had never pass'd away:
I could not draw my een from theirs**184**
  Ne turn them up to pray.

And in its time the spell was snapt,
  And I could move my een:
I look'd far-forth, but little saw
  Of what might else be seen.   450

Like one, that on a lonely road
  Doth walk in fear and dread,
And having once turn'd round, walks on
  And turns no more his head:
Because he knows, a frightful fiend
  Doth close behind him tread.

But soon there breath'd a wind on me,
  Ne sound ne motion made:
Its path was not upon the sea
  In ripple or in shade.   460

It rais'd my hair, it fann'd my cheek,
  Like a meadow-gale of spring—
It mingled strangely with my fears,
  Yet it felt like a welcoming.

Swiftly, swiftly flew the ship,
  Yet she sail'd softly too:
Sweetly, sweetly blew the breeze—
  On me alone it blew.

O dream of joy! is this indeed
  The light-house top I see?   470
Is this the Hill? Is this the Kirk?
  Is this mine own countrée?

We drifted o'er the Harbour-bar,
  And I with sobs did pray—
"O let me be awake, my God!
  "Or let me sleep alway!"

The harbour-bay was clear as glass,
  So smoothly it was strewn!
And on the bay the moon light lay,
  And the shadow of the moon.   480

184. Een: Eyes.

And on the bay the moonlight lay,
And the shadow of the Moon.

The moonlight bay was white all o'er,
  Till rising from the same,
Full many shapes, that shadows were,
  Like as of torches came.

A little distance from the prow
  Those dark-red shadows were;
But soon I saw that my own flesh
  Was red as in a glare.

I turn'd my head in fear and dread,
  And by the holy rood,   490
The bodies had advanc'd, and now
  Before the mast they stood.

They lifted up their stiff right arms,
  They held them strait and tight;
And each right-arm burnt like a torch,
  A torch that's borne upright.
Their stony eye-balls glitter'd on
  In the red and smoky light.**185**

I pray'd and turn'd my head away
  Forth looking as before.   500
There was no breeze upon the bay,
  No wave against the shore.

The rock shone bright, the kirk no less
  That stands above the rock:
The moonlight steep'd in silentness
  The steady weathercock.

185. Lowes believes (See his Note 60 to Chap. XV) that the flaming right arms of the corpses may have been suggested to Coleridge by an old superstition known as the "Hand of Glory." According to this belief, if a hand is cut from the corpse of a hanged man, then prepared in certain mysterious ways, it functions as a powerful talisman. In some cases the hand, after being set on fire like a torch, has the power of temporarily paralyzing anyone who views the flame. Lowes gives many references to the superstition, but says that the most interesting account of it is in Chapter 24, "The Hand of Glory," in Sabine Baring-Gould's novel, *Red Spider*. Coleridge probably decided that the entire stanza, like his stanza describing the black skeleton of Death in Part III, was too gruesome. At any rate, he later removed it from the poem.

Full many shapes, that shadows were,
In crimson colors came.

And the bay was white with silent light,
  Till rising from the same
Full many shapes, that shadows were,
  In crimson colours came.   510

A little distance from the prow
  Those crimson shadows were:
I turn'd my eyes upon the deck—
  O Christ! what saw I there?

Each corse lay flat, lifeless and flat;
  And by the Holy rood
A man all light, a seraph-man,
  On every corse there stood.

This seraph-band, each wav'd his hand:
  It was a heavenly sight: 520
They stood as signals to the land,
  Each one a lovely light:

This seraph-band, each wav'd his hand,
  No voice did they impart—
No voice; but O! the silence sank,
  Like music on my heart.

Eftsones I heard the dash of oars,**186**
  I heard the pilot's cheer:
My head was turn'd perforce away
  And I saw a boat appear.   530

186. Eftsones: Immediately. In 1800 Coleridge removed this word from the stanza. In 1802 he added it to the third stanza of Part I, its spelling altered to "eftsoons."

This seraph-band, each waved his hand:
It was a heavenly sight!

Then vanish'd all the lovely lights;
    The bodies rose anew:
With silent pace, each to his place,
    Came back the ghastly crew.
The wind, that shade nor motion made,
    On me alone it blew.**187**

The pilot, and the pilot's boy
    I heard them coming fast:
Dear Lord in Heaven! it was a joy,
    The dead men could not blast.   540

I saw a third—I heard his voice:
    It is the Hermit good!
He singeth loud his godly hymns
    That he makes in the wood.
He'll shrieve my soul, he'll wash away
    The Albatross's blood.

187. In a copy of *Lyrical Ballads,* Coleridge wrote the following variant of this stanza:

> Then vanish'd all the lovely lights,
>   The spirits of the air,
> No souls of mortal men were they,
>   But spirits bright and fair.

He later decided, however, to drop the entire stanza except for its last line, "On me alone it blew," which appears as line 463 in the ballad's final version.

VII

This Hermit good lives in that wood
   Which slopes down to the Sea.
How loudly his sweet voice he rears!
He loves to talk with Marineres   550
   That come from a far Countrée.

He kneels at morn and noon and eve—
   He hath a cushion plump:
It is the moss, that wholly hides
   The rotted old Oak-stump.

The Skiff-boat ne'rd: I heard them talk,
   "Why, this is strange, I trow!
"Where are those lights so many and fair
   "That signal made but now?"

"Strange, by my faith!" the Hermit said—   560
   "And they answer'd not our cheer.
"The planks look warp'd, and see those sails
   "How thin they are and sere!
"I never saw aught like to them
   "Unless perchance it were

"The skeletons of leaves that lag
   "My forest-brook along:
"When the Ivy-tod is heavy with snow,
"And the Owlet whoops to the wolf below
   "That eats the she-wolf's young."   570

"Dear Lord! it has a fiendish look—"
   (The Pilot made reply)
"I am afear'd—" "Push on, push on!"
   Said the Hermit cheerily.

The Boat came closer to the Ship,
   But I ne spake ne stirr'd!
The Boat came close beneath the Ship.
   And strait a sound was heard!

Under the water it rumbled on,
   Still louder and more dread: 580
It reach'd the Ship, it split the bay;
   The Ship went down like lead.

Under the water it rumbled on,
Still louder and more dread.

Upon the whirl, where sank the ship,
The boat spun round and round.

Stunn'd by that loud and dreadful sound,
  Which sky and ocean smote:
Like one that had been seven days drown'd
  My body lay afloat:
But, swift as dreams, myself I found
  Within the Pilot's boat.

Upon the whirl, where sank the Ship,
  The boat spun round and round: 590
And all was still, save that the hill
  Was telling of the sound.

I mov'd my lips: the Pilot shriek'd
  And fell down in a fit.
The Holy Hermit rais'd his eyes
  And pray'd where he did sit.

I took the oars: the Pilot's boy,
  Who now doth crazy go,
Laugh'd loud and long, and all the while
  His eyes went to and fro,   600
"Ha! ha!" quoth he—"full plain I see,
  "The devil knows how to row."

And now all in mine own Countrée
  I stood on the firm land!
The Hermit stepp'd forth from the boat,
  And scarcely he could stand.

"O shrieve me, shrieve me, holy Man!"
  The Hermit cross'd his brow—
"Say quick," quoth he, "I bid thee say
  "What manner man art thou?"   610

Forthwith this frame of mine was wrench'd
  With a woeful agony,
Which forc'd me to begin my tale
  And then it left me free.

Since then at an uncertain hour,
  Now oftimes and now fewer,
That anguish comes and makes me tell
  My ghastly aventure.

I pass, like night, from land to land;
  I have strange power of speech;   620
The moment that his face I see
I know the man that must hear me;
  To him my tale I teach.

160

I moved my lips—the Pilot shrieked
And fell down in a fit.

"O shrieve me, shrieve me, holy man!"

I pass, like night, from land to land;
I have strange power of speech.

That moment that his face I see,
I know the man that must hear me.

What loud uproad bursts from that door!
  The Wedding-guests are there;
But in the Garden-bower the Bride
  And Bride-maids singing are:
And hark the little Vesper-bell
  Which biddeth me to prayer.

O Wedding-guest! this soul hath been   630
  Alone on a wide wide sea:
So lonely 'twas, that God himself
  Scarce seemed there to be.

O sweeter than the Marriage-feast,
  'This sweeter far to me
To walk together to the Kirk
  With a goodly company.

To walk together to the Kirk
  And all together pray,
While each to his great Father bends,   640
Old men, and babes, and loving friends,
  And Youths, and Maidens gay.

Farewell, farewell! but this I tell
  To thee, thou wedding-guest!
He prayeth well who loveth well
  Both man and bird and beast.

He prayeth best who loveth best,
  All things both great and small:
For the dear God, who loveth us,
  He made and loveth all.   650

The Marinere, whose eye is bright,
  Whose beard with age is hoar,
Is gone; and now the wedding-guest
  Turn'd from the bridegroom's door.

He went, like one that hath been stunn'd
  And is of sense forlorn:
A sadder and a wiser man
  He rose the morrow morn.

What loud uproar bursts from that door!
The wedding-guests are there.

So lonely 'twas, that God himself
Scarce seemed there to be.

The Mariner, whose eye is bright,
Whose beard with age is hoar,
Is gone.

PART IV

Interpretations

"A poem," so runs a much quoted line by Archibald MacLeish, "should not mean but be." It is a puzzling statement. How can a poem, unless it means something, possibly "be"? Other types of art are quite different. A symphony doesn't have to mean anything; the listener has a direct, pleasurable experience of the sounds. An abstract painting doesn't have to mean anything; it is just there, a created, palpable object to be observed and enjoyed. But a poem has to be communicated by queer little black marks on white paper, the marks arranged in complicated patterns that give no aesthetic pleasure in themselves. The patterns are visual symbols understood only by a person with a sensitive memory of how his culture attributes sounds and meanings to those patterns. Without these sounds and meanings, there is no poem.

Nevertheless, MacLeish's line does make a significant point. The little black marks are not the poem. They are no more than patterns employed to symbolize the poem. After one has interpreted these patterns as best he can, drawing upon all the subtle sounds and meanings that a culture has bestowed on them, the poem itself—the real poem—takes shape as a constructed object, a thing (even though it exists only in his mind) that can be directly experienced in a way not much different from the way in which one experiences a symphony or a painting. When that stage is reached, the poem ceases to be something that must be explained; it becomes an art object to be experienced.

The purpose of this book is to help the reader reach such a stage with respect to one poem. Up to this point, our attempts to explicate Coleridge's ballad have been relatively superficial: defining words and phrases, clarifying obscurities that have arisen because we are not living in early nineteenth-century England, and pointing out subtleties of meaning probably intended by the poet but easily missed unless the poem is read many times and thought about deeply. The notes have also touched occasionally on the techniques by which Coleridge strengthened the vividness and emotional impact of his lines. We have seen how he chose the old English ballad form to convey the feel of an ancient time; how he borrowed from this form its use of repetition, alliteration, elemental imagery, color, and archaic diction. We have seen how he avoided the rigidity of the old ballad form by skillfully varying its rhythms and the number of lines in its stanzas, whenever such departures contributed to a desired effect. Above all, we have seen how Coleridge, with his great sensitivity to the rich overtones of English, chose his words and phrases, and put them together in such a way, as to arouse intensely vivid pictures in the mind. It is this extraordinary power of Coleridge that provides the sheer "magic" quality of the poem. (No other adjective has been more often applied to it.) Disbelief in the Mariner's preposterous tale is momentarily put aside; one almost *sees* the fire-flags and the water snakes, the helmsman's face illuminated by the lamp, the motionless weathercock, the blood-red sun, the stony, glittering eyes of the dead men. No English poem before or since has been capable of arousing, for so many readers, such intense images of unearthly beauty and terror.

Moreover, there is a curious way in which the imagery of a great poem such as this grows even more intense with the passage of time. Its lines and episodes work their way into the literature of a culture; they are quoted, borrowed, and echoed by later poets and writers. There is a kind of feedback. When we read a poem that has become a classic, its lines reverberate with subliminally comprehended overtones that derive from later works of literature. Every great poem suffers an inevitable erosion of meaning with the passage of years, as language and customs and values change; but at the same time, every great poem accumulates new meanings. In some respects *The Ancient Mariner* can be read today with greater pleasure than it could in Coleridge's time.

A few notes have pointed out ways in which events in Coleridge's life, and aspects of his personality, may have colored the meanings of certain lines. Though such biographical analysis is often considered superficial, it does add something, however small, to the total meaning of a poem. Hugh I'Anson Fausset's *Samuel Taylor Coleridge* (1926) devotes a chapter to *The Ancient Mariner* in which this approach is stressed. When the Mariner speaks of passing like night from land to land, with his strange power of speech, Fausset sees Coleridge himself, "longing to escape from the solitude of an abnormal consciousness, seeking relief throughout his life in endless monologues." When the Mariner speaks of walking to the kirk as sweeter than the marriage feast, is Coleridge thinking of "his own never-satisfied need of simple, devout human relationships . . ."? Is the stanza that begins "Oh sleep! it is a gentle thing," an expression of the poet's physical indolence? Is the moral ("He prayeth best . . .") an expression of "his own childlike affection for everything without distinction"? And so on. Fausset is convinced that it is because Coleridge projected his own hopes and terrors so completely into this ballad that it acquired more "reality" than his other poems and became his greatest poem.

Lowes's approach to the ballad, in *The Road to Xanadu*, is also essentially biographical. As the reader surely knows, this famous tour-de-force of English criticism is an exhaustive genetic study of the ballad's literary sources. Following up clues in Coleridge's notebooks and letters, Lowes set himself the task of trying to read everything that Coleridge was known to have read before he wrote the poem, as well as books he probably read or even *might* have read. This literary detective work paid off handsomely, for it turned out that Coleridge had borrowed heavily, often exact words and phrases, from the leading sea travel books of the time. The more important of these borrowings have been cited in our notes.

In his omnivorous reading of travel books, Coleridge always read with what Lowes called the poet's "falcon eye," searching for just those details which could best be transmuted into poetry. But Lowes believed that these details worked their way into Coleridge's unconscious and pre-conscious where they lay dormant until he began the actual writing of his ballad. Then, by those obscure processes of association which had been detailed and analyzed by David Hartley, memories of what he read fused together in his conscious mind and emerged in lines of the ballad. Maybe so. I am inclined, however, to suspect that it was all more conscious than Lowes would have us believe. There is no reason why Coleridge, when he reached the point at which he wanted to describe the colors of icebergs, could not have flipped through the pages of a travel book until he found, say, the phrase "green as emerald." "Perfect!" he shouts. "Just what I've been looking for!"

This is the point of view taken by Robert Cecil Bald in his important paper, "The Ancient Mariner: Addenda to *The Road to Xanadu*," in *Nineteenth Century Studies* (1940). Coleridge's reading, says Bald (drawing on data from notebooks not available to Lowes), was not as random as Lowes proposes. One of Coleridge's notes is: "To read most carefully for the purposes of poetry" an account of an earthquake. Coleridge may have been fully aware of how much he had borrowed from the travel books.

Evaluating the influence of opium on Coleridge's poems is also part of a biographical approach. Here, too, Bald takes issue with Lowes. Lowes played down the effects of the drug. John M. Robertson, in *New Essays Toward a Critical Method* (1897), and Meyer H. Abrams, in *The Milk of Paradise* (1934), play up the drug. Bald steers a middle course. He reasons, quite sensibly, that although Coleridge may not have been strongly addicted to opium at the time he wrote *The Ancient Mariner,* he may have been sufficiently addicted to experience the milder reveries. Perhaps in 1800, when he added the subtitle "A Poet's Reverie" to the ballad, he was thinking of opium reveries. Perhaps one reason he seized upon the plot, when it was suggested by a neighbor's dream, was because he saw at once that here was a magnificent outlet for the vivid dream phenomena that had been building up in his mind. There is no way to be sure, but this view seems plausible.

Another important biographical fact, already mentioned in the notes, is that Coleridge had never been to sea when he first wrote his ballad. During World War II, I served in the North Atlantic on a destroyer escort, a ship small enough so that a sailor could really get to know the sea in a way quite different from that of the tourist who floats gently over the ocean on a huge hotel. I can assure the reader that the smell of the sea is not in the first version of Coleridge's poem. This is not to say that the poem does not convey a strong sense of reality, but only to say that it is not the real sea that Coleridge makes seem real. It is a fantasy sea. There is less of the true sea in the entire ballad than in a dozen lines that one can find on hundreds of pages by Melville or Conrad, or in Masefield's single line: "And the flung spray and the blown spume and the seagulls crying." "This great sea-piece might have had more in it of the air and savour of the sea," wrote Swinburne (discussing the poem in *Memories and Studies*). David Hartley's doctrine of association of ideas explains, of course, why the sea's savor never entered the poem's first version: Coleridge had never savored it.

As Bald points out, Coleridge later *did* go to sea, and then he did add to his ballad some passages which more strongly convey a sense of actual sea life. For example, the lines about the sloping masts of the ship as the storm blast drives it forward, and the description of the helmsman's face lit at night by his lamp. (There is a notebook entry, No. 2001, in which Coleridge records having observed the second scene.) But even with these welcome additions, the ship remains largely a painted ship on a painted ocean.

An attempt to probe deeper into the influence on the poem of

Interpretations

Coleridge's life and character has been made by David Beres in his paper, "A Dream, a Vision, and a Poem" (*International Journal of Psycho-Analysis*, Vol. 32, Part 2, 1951). As far as I know, it remains the only attempt by a professional analyst to explicate the poem by way of Freudian insights and symbols. Coleridge's many references in his writings to food and hunger, his strong desire to be loved, his preoccupation with sleep and dreams, his "devouring" of books, and so on, lead Beres to conclude that Coleridge was an almost clinically perfect instance of what the Freudians call an oral character. In addition, he finds evidence that early in life Coleridge developed an ambivalent attitude toward his mother, failed to resolve his infantile aggression, became confused as to his sexual identity. He sees Coleridge's relationships with his male friends, especially Wordsworth, as unconsciously homosexual.[1] The poet's inability to resolve his sense of guilt toward his mother thus underlies his unhappy love life, his steadily increasing depression and anxiety, and his dependence on opium as a relief from suffering.

How accurate this picture is, I am not prepared to say. Beres advanced it tentatively, before he had access to Coleridge's notebooks, now being published. In many ways the picture seems accurate, though a careful student of Coleridge is likely to suspect that the poet's character is less simple than Beres makes it out to be. I will cite only one instance of how easy it is to misinterpret biographical details. Coleridge's poem "Dejection: An Ode" is a moving expression of grief, despair, and a sense of one's creative powers slowly being drained away. "It cannot be without significance," writes Beres, "that this poem was written on the occasion of Wordsworth's marriage to Mary Hutchinson, an added hint of Coleridge's unconscious homosexual attachment to his friend." But the poem was *not* written on the occasion of Wordsworth's marriage; it just happened to be *published* in a newspaper on the day of the marriage. It was written six months before Wordsworth's marriage, and has long been known to be an expression of Coleridge's hopeless, unrequited love for Sarah Hutchinson. The published version was care-

---

1. "I believe it possible that a man may, under certain states of the moral feeling, entertain something deserving the name of love towards a male object—an affection beyond friendship, and wholly aloof from appetite." Havelock Ellis quotes this passage (from Coleridge's *Table Talk,* May 14, 1833) in his book on *Sexual Inversion* and comments: "This passage of Coleridge's is interesting as an early English recognition by a distinguished man of genius of what may be termed ideal homosexuality."

fully cut and edited to conceal the true source of his grief, but the original version of the poem, which he sent in a letter to Sarah, has been known since 1937 when it was first printed by Ernest de Selincourt. (Selincourt later included it in his *Wordsworthian and Other Studies,* 1947. It may also be found in George Whalley's *Coleridge and Sara Hutchinson,* 1955, and Humphry House's *Coleridge,* 1953.) One could scarcely find a more "clinically perfect" description of that drained, empty feeling of a man who has come to realize that a love for a certain woman is not, and will not, be returned. It was not Coleridge, but Dorothy Wordsworth who was most upset by her brother's marriage.

It is harder to take seriously Beres's symbolic interpretation of *The Ancient Mariner.* The albatross naturally is regarded as a symbol of Coleridge's mother, providing the poet an outlet for his repressed hostility. The Mariner's crime is mother-murder, carrying with it, according to Beres, an unconscious incest motive. (For Kenneth Burke, in *Philosophy of Literary Form,* the bird is a symbol of Coleridge's wife. Beres would probably agree, for he regards the wife herself as another mother symbol.) His punishment is hunger, loss of love, and loneliness: "pregenital punishments for a preoedipal crime." The mother image appears again in the ballad as the avenging spectre-woman, Life-in-Death, then finally as the forgiving Holy Mother who sends rain and sleep. "The mother whom he restores to life brings him back to the safety of his homeland. A mother-figure forgives the crime against the mother."

With this background, Beres has little difficulty interpreting numerous lines in ways that reinforce his central theme. Consider the "silly buckets on the deck" (line 297). Beres points out that according to the *Shorter Oxford Dictionary* the meaning of "silly" is "feeble, frail, insignificant." He concludes: "It is not too rash an assumption that the buckets symbolize the mother's breasts, previously empty and cruel, now full and forgiving."

Well, perhaps a *bit* rash? This is not meant to question the soundness of Beres's over-all analysis of Coleridge's character, but to question the degree to which unconscious symbolic meanings can be made specific in a fantasy poem so rich in symbolic possibilities. Rules for the interpretation of literary symbols, in the Freudian school, are so loose and uncontrolled that attempts at such interpretation easily degenerate into a clever game based largely on word puns and visual similarities. The game is so easy to play that it becomes almost valueless in providing reinforcement for a character interpretation.

Interpretations

Let the reader try the following experiment. Pick at random any type of neurotic personality. Then go over *The Ancient Mariner* carefully, searching for symbols to reinforce the traits of the chosen personality. He will be amazed at how readily the symbols turn up. The point is not that a poem cannot contain unconscious symbolic expressions of the poet's hopes, fears, and conflicts, but that it is rash to regard the finding of such symbols as confirming evidence for previously made character assumptions. Analysts who play this game with literature seem to have little awareness of how fantastically flexible are the controls on this kind of feedback—so flexible, in fact, that it is impossible to lose.

For example, if Coleridge had spoken of the albatross as "her," Beres would have considered this supporting evidence for his central thesis. But Coleridge speaks of the bird as "him" (line 405). No matter—one wins either way. "To Coleridge," writes Beres, in accounting for the "him," "the father was a feminine, giving male; the mother a masculine, rejecting female." Had Coleridge not specified the bird's sex, this too would do the trick, for was not the mother an ambivalent sexual figure? The Freudian critic first makes a tentative hypothesis about a poet's neuroses, he searches for symbols in the poet's writings that fit the hypothesis, then the symbols are taken as confirming evidence for the hypothesis. I do not here attack the value of the hypothesis; I merely suggest (in a whisper) that Freudian symbolic interpretation is so elastic and uncontrolled that the support it provides for character analysis is largely a mirage. This is especially true with respect to a fantasy poem in which there are hundreds of possible symbols, each capable of many interpretations.

The analytic tradition, on its Jungian side, provides the background for Maud Bodkin's symbolic approach to *The Ancient Mariner* in her path-breaking study, *Archetypal Patterns in Poetry* (1934). Miss Bodkin is less concerned with the poem as an expression of Coleridge's neuroses than with the poem as an expression of certain universal emotional patterns that are inescapable aspects of human nature itself, as distinct from less basic emotions that may vary from time to time, culture to culture, person to person. She reasons that, when a poem continues to fascinate and deeply move large numbers of readers for more than a century, it must deal with emotional themes of great universality— themes that are permanently impressed upon the reader's unconscious. From Jung she borrows the term "archetype" as a name for such a theme, and with this she also takes over, though with cerain reservations and doubts, Jung's belief in a "collective unconscious."

175

THE ANNOTATED ANCIENT MARINER

Both Freud and Jung were firmly convinced that the human mind, at birth, has stamped upon its neural circuits various patterns of behavior and emotional response that are records of the collective experience of countless ancestors. This aspect of the analytic movement has today been abandoned (except for a few old-fashioned fundamentalists) but in 1934, when Miss Bodkin published her book, the anthropological evidence was only starting to pour in, and the revisionary work of the more progressive analysts was only beginning. It is to Miss Bodkin's credit that she was well enough acquainted with the anthropological evidence to admit that there was no empirical support for Jung's collective unconscious, and that it might be possible to explain the universality and persistence of archetypal patterns in terms of a common cultural heritage and common aspects of human experience. Of course it is possible. The entire biological background of Miss Bodkin's book can be discarded with no loss whatever to her critical positions.

Consider, for example, the archetype that she finds central to the emotional power of *The Ancient Mariner:* the theme of death and rebirth. The Mariner commits a senseless crime, a "hellish thing." It results in the death of all his shipmates, and plunges him into physical suffering and mental agony. He finds himself alone on a rotting sea, dying of thirst, surrounded by a thousand thousand slimy things. He tries to pray, but his heart is as dry as his throat. "The imagery of calm and drought here," writes R. L. Brett in *Reason and Imagination* (1960), "is as old as religious poetry itself. From the valley of dry bones in the Book of Ezekiel to Eliot's *The Waste Land,* dryness has symbolized spiritual barrenness. . . ."

Then comes the turning point, that great somersault of faith so cleverly symbolized by Dante when, at the exact center of the earth, he turns himself upside down and begins the slow climb from hell to purgatory. The Mariner's heart goes out in love toward God and nature. He is suddenly able to pray. The albatross, symbol of his burden of guilt, drops from his neck. The gentle peace of heaven slides into his soul, and when he awakes, rain assuages his great thirst. The ship starts its mysterious motion that carries him home:

> But soon there breathed a wind on me,
> Nor sound nor motion made:
> Its path was not upon the sea,
> In ripple or in shade.

> It raised my hair, it fanned my cheek
> Like a meadow-gale of spring—
> It mingled strangely with my fears,
> Yet it felt like a welcoming.

The poem is thus an allegory in the higher sense in which certain Greeks myths may be considered allegorical. Coleridge himself, in his criticism, stressed the difference between what he called an allegory— a story in which every object and incident is symbolic of something else—and a symbolic narrative in which only certain objects and incidents give to the story, in an overall way, a universal meaning. The ballad, in short, is a myth. It is more like, say, *Moby Dick* than *Pilgrim's Progress* or *The Faerie Queene*. It can be read, understood, and enjoyed solely as a narrative, but after many readings and much reflection, a higher level of significance forms above the narrative like a luminous cloud.

There is little doubt that a major source of the ballad's emotional power is this rebirth pattern of sin-suffering-death-repentance-rebirth-penance-salvation. But there is no need to invoke the Lamarckian views of nineteenth-century biologists to explain the power of such a pattern. Not only is it one of the central myths of Christianity, the shreds of which are still firmly a part of the West's cultural heritage, but the bare bones of the rebirth theme are inescapable in every man's experience. Each night we lapse into unconsciousness, a death of many hours, to find ourselves reborn the following morning. Every year we see the wintry deaths of trees and plants followed by their spring rebirths. We take to bed with an illness, we recover. Older generations pass away, the young take over. Life is filled with cycles of death and renewal. There is no need to invent a process by which collective memories of the dead are recorded inside our skulls. The experience of every child before the age of ten, in Manhattan or Africa, is sufficient to account for the mind's response to the rebirth archetype in literature.

A child who grows up with a Protestant or Catholic background learns, of course, versions of the rebirth pattern that have the more specific form which Coleridge's ballad dramatizes. This is true even in liberal Protestant churches where the minister and most of his congregation do not believe in the Resurrection of Christ or that conversion is a transfer from a road leading to eternal damnation to a road leading to eternal happiness. On Easter Sunday even a Unitarian minister, a bit embarrassed by the larger church attendance, inevitably finds himself speaking in symbols of death and rebirth. A child who attends a more traditional Protestant church will sing hymns, some of them dating back to Coleridge's time, which exploit symbols virtually identical with some of the rebirth symbols in *The Ancient Mariner*. The "going home" theme is central to hundreds of hymns. Some even identify the lost soul with a mariner lost at sea:

> My soul in sad exile was out on life's sea,
>> So burdened with sin and distressed,
> Till I heard a sweet voice saying, "Make me your choice,"
>> And I entered the haven of rest.

Another source of the ballad's emotional power is, one suspects, its exploitation of an archetype even older and more pervasive than the rebirth pattern. I refer to the concept of the supernatural, the myth of Plato's cave, the conviction that the world we know is a shadow world. Behind it, hidden from us, is another, wholly other world. Coleridge's quotation from Burnet, which heads his poem, speaks of exactly this. The ballad is a Platonic poem, suffused throughout with that *mysterium tremendum* that lies at the heart of all the world's great religious faiths. The poem's horrors are the horrors of this world. Is the silent, rotting sea more ghastly than the steady-state universe of a modern naturalist, endlessly repeating more of the same, in all directions, throughout eternity, like one of those mad, meaningless machines that mechanics sometimes build as a joke? It is this transcendent blankness, this absolute nothingness surrounding the universe, that is the ultimate repressed horror of modern Aristotelianism. It is the Platonic dualism, the intimation of a higher reality—albeit one filled with angels and water daemons—that is the huge and omnipresent archetypal pattern of Coleridge's ballad.

Throughout the poem Coleridge plays with this and other archetypal themes, and with words and images that in themselves, like the words of the King James Bible or a good folk song, are archetypal and eternal: wind, rain, sun, moon, star, sleep, soul, love, life, death. Miss Bodkin's book devotes several memorable pages to analyzing the emotional effect of "red" in that wonderful stanza:

> Her beams bemocked the sultry main,
>> Like April hoar-frost spread;
> But where the ship's huge shadow lay,
> The charméd water burnt alway
>> A still and awful red.

Interpretations

"There is, I suspect," wrote Lowes, "no magic in the poem more potent than this blending of images through which the glowing redness of animalcules once seen in the Pacific has imbued with sombre mystery that still and boding sea and the image which lies across it with utter distinctness in a hush of brooding light."

Why does this simple three-letter word "red" hit the reader with such force? Because, suggests Miss Bodkin, "The word 'red' has a soul of terror that has come to it through the history of the race." Yes, but the Jungian racial memory is wholly unnecessary to explain it. Before a child talks he has associated red with the color of blood and fire; before he is a young man he has associated it with a girl's lips, the signal light of danger, the scarlet woman, painting the town red. In the Soviet Union it is the color of revolution. In Christian nations it is the color of Satan, the hats of cardinals, the blood of the communion service. "Red," writes G. K. Chesterton ("The Red Town" in *Alarms and Discursions*), "is the most joyful and dreadful thing in the physical universe; it is the fiercest note, it is the highest light, it is the place where the walls of this world of ours wear thinnest and something beyond burns through."

No poet was ever more sensitive to the overtones of color words than Coleridge. Who doubts that he could have talked for hours about the "hooks and eyes of the memory" (as he once called the laws of association) by which the word "red" is linked with human experience? This word and its synonyms appear more frequently in *The Ancient Mariner* than any other color word. Miss Bodkin says she cannot read Coleridge's line about the ship's awful shadow without thinking of Dante's city of Dis, its red mosques glowing in a dark valley of the Inferno. She has given a valuable account of her own free associations and deeply felt emotions when she reads *The Ancient Mariner*—an account that will enrich any reader's understanding of the ballad—but Jung's collective unconscious is utterly irrelevant to her central theme.

Miss Bodkin, as well as many later myth critics, often gives the impression that Coleridge's powerful elemental words and archetypal patterns entered his work unconsciously. This is hard to believe. Certainly the archetype of death and rebirth, in its Christian trappings, was deliberately and skillfully woven into the Mariner's tale. Young Coleridge, the son of a vicar, must have heard countless sermons on death and resurrection, and the miraculous conversion of sinners. We know from his letters, written during the year that preceded the writing of his ballad, that he was intensely preoccupied with original sin, repentance,

179

and the nature of the Fall, and that his views were moving rapidly from Unitarianism back to orthodoxy. In "The Eolian Harp," a poem written two years before *The Ancient Mariner*, he speaks of himself as a "sinful and most miserable man" who had been healed and given peace by the saving mercies of the "Incomprehensible." Before writing his ballad he had planned an epic poem on the origin of evil. Most critics assume that this was his projected poem, "The Wanderings of Cain," which he did not finish because, as he tells us, he wrote *The Ancient Mariner* instead. It is impossible to suppose he could have written those stanzas about the mysterious wind that breathed on the Mariner without full conscious awareness of the wind as a Biblical symbol of the Holy Spirit.

We can go further. *The Ancient Mariner* swarms with other religious symbols, not part of the rebirth archetype but so common in the religious literature and sermonizing of Coleridge's time that he could not have escaped recognizing them. How could he, for example, not have realized that the murder of the albatross carried emotional associations with the murder of Christ? We are told that the Polar Spirit "loved the bird that loved the man/Who shot him with his bow." No one with Coleridge's background and faith could fail to see here an analogy with God who loved His Son who loved the men who pierced him. The line just quoted is spoken by a daemon who a moment before had used the phrase, "By Him who died on cross." It is no accident, or upwelling of Coleridge's pre-conscious, that the albatross is hung on the Mariner's neck like a crucifix. Even the "cross" in "cross-bow" suggests the murder weapon with which Jesus was killed. I do not say that Coleridge worked out a vast, intricate, self-consistent metaphorical level for every stanza of his poem, or even that his Mariner was intended throughout as a symbol of all men, on the great sea voyage of life, burdened by Original Sin until they repent and are reborn. I do say that the Christian symbolism of the poem is so pervasive and obvious, the symbols so much a part of English Protestant culture in the late eighteenth century, that Coleridge would have had to have been simple-minded not to be aware of them in his ballad.

When we turn from the Christian theme of guilt and rebirth to subsidiary symbolic meanings of the ballad, we at once enter choppier waters. Coleridge did not leave a detailed analysis of his symbolic intent, and we can only speculate when we try to distinguish between the following three levels:

1. Symbols consciously employed.

2. Symbols unconsciously or semi-consciously used, but nevertheless legitimate "meanings" of the poem.

3. Symbols not intended in either of the above senses, but which the poem has acquired almost by accident as the lines are given interpretations by later readers.

Of course there are no sharp lines separating the three levels. If you ask a poet whether he intended a certain symbolic meaning, he may answer, with complete honesty, that he doesn't know. He may have been dissatisfied with the awkward rhythms of a certain line. In altering the words he suddenly thought of an entirely new line, of great verbal beauty. While writing it down he is startled to recognize that it has a symbolic meaning in harmony with the rest of the poem. Was this symbolic meaning "intended"? How can the poet himself say? It is consciously intended in the sense that, having written the line, he is aware of its symbolic meaning, approves of it, and lets the line stay. It is not consciously intended in the sense that he did not seek for such a symbol, but only recognized it after he wrote it down. Was it unconsciously intended? Who can tell? It may have been a wholly accidental by-product of a search for a musical phrase; yet it certainly becomes a legitimate part of the poem's total meaning. Consider that well-known couplet of identical lines closing Robert Frost's "Stopping by Woods on a Snowy Evening":

> And miles to go before I sleep,
> And miles to go before I sleep.

It is difficult not to read the first line literally and its repetition as a symbolic reference to the Big Sleep. Yet we have Frost's own word for it that he did not intend this meaning when he wrote the poem, although he did admit once in a lecture that he had "the feeling" that his poem was "loaded with ulteriority." It is quite possible that Frost did not even unconsciously intend sleep as a symbol of death. But who would wish to eliminate this as one of the poem's meanings? Who would wish to discard the symbolic meanings that have been bestowed on passages in Homer? Every fantasy poem is so crowded with potential symbols that the probability of *some* accidental meanings, in harmony with the poem's central theme, is almost certain; but the difficulty of distinguishing this third level of meaning from the other two becomes very great indeed.

Physicists have a rule that if there are no laws to prevent something from happening in nature, it will. In poetic criticism there is a similar rule: If there is any possible attitude to take toward a great poem, some critic is sure to take it. *The Ancient Mariner* is no exception. It may be that no poem of comparable shortness has been subjected to so many varying symbolic interpretations.

Many critics view the poem as essentially a narrative about supernatural events that occur during a sea voyage, with few or no intended higher levels of meaning. True, Coleridge added an explicit moral at the end, almost as an afterthought, but (say these critics) he did not intend his ballad to carry the weight of vast symbolic meanings, and little is gained in searching for them. It may be that here and there he intended a stanza to be symbolic, but on the whole, no higher metaphysical theme was part of the poet's intent. This is more or less the point of view of Lowes, Elisabeth Schneider (in *Coleridge, Opium and Kubla Khan*), Earl Leslie Griggs (in *The Best of Coleridge*), John Muirhead (in *Coleridge as Philosopher*), and many other critics.

At the other extreme are various attempts to treat the ballad as a carefully worked out allegory in which every character, object, and event is designed to carry a symbolic meaning that contributes to the higher theme. An early specimen of this approach is Gertrude Garrogues' paper, "Coleridge's 'Ancient Mariner,'" in the *Journal of Speculative Philosophy*, July, 1880. She regards the poem as throughout, stanza by stanza, a carefully planned allegory of the Christian theme of sin and redemption. Why does the Mariner stoppeth one of three? Because, as the Bible tells us, many are called but few are chosen; not every person is prepared to receive the story of salvation. Why is the sun above the mast at noon? Because the Mariner has finished the merry childhood of his voyage through life and has now reached maturity. And so on. The ballad is, thinks the author, the closest Coleridge ever came to writing that great work on Christian philosophy about which he talked so much!

There are many good things in Miss Garrogues' article, but, of course, she goes too far. I myself believe that the religious rebirth theme, in its Christian form, was consciously intended by Coleridge as the binding theme of his narrative, but surely not in a line-by-line way. It is likely that Coleridge himself was not fully aware of the extent of this theme when he first wrote the ballad. As Marius Bewley has said, only in "odd corners" of the poem can one feel fairly certain that the theme was intended. In his later changes, especially in the addition of the gloss,

Coleridge sought to strengthen this theme and make it more apparent to the reader. But much of the action is hard to fit into any detailed allegory, and most critics who accept the poem as a Christian myth are careful not to press their metaphors too far. Like the Freudian symbol game, this religious symbol game is also easy to play.

One of the most perplexing problems, for readers who accept the sin and redemption theme, is to account for the apparent senselessness of the Mariner's crime. At the time Coleridge wrote the ballad he was well on his way toward the abandonment of Hartley's necessitarianism; there are many reasons to suppose that he intended the Mariner's lack of motive to dramatize an act that sprang directly from original sin. "A sin is an evil which has its ground or origin in the agent, and not in the compulsion of circumstances," he wrote many years later in *Aids to Reflection*. A man who commits a crime under the pressure of outer events is not really sinning in the deepest sense; he "may feel regret, but cannot feel remorse . . ." Original sin, he goes on to say, is a profound mystery which we cannot hope to understand. "It follows necessarily from the postulate of a responsible will. Refuse to grant this, and I have not a word to say. Concede this and you concede all . . ."

If those were Coleridge's sentiments when he wrote his ballad, as I suspect they were, then the Mariner's motiveless cruelty may have a symbolic meaning essential to the poem's religious theme. The shooting of the albatross, like the shooting of President Kennedy, is banal and idiotic, more in keeping with Dante's imbecilic, three-headed Satan than Milton's proud, handsome, understandable, and in some ways admirable arch-fiend. The really great sinner, Dante and Coleridge seem to be saying, is simply a fool. He wills his crime, knowing it a crime, but wills it for no particular reason.

C. M. Bowra, in his excellent chapter on *The Ancient Mariner* (in *The Romantic Imagination*, 1949), gives a well-balanced defense of the Christian theme. "We may begin by asking, as others have," he writes, "why there is all this 'pother about a bird,' but we end by seeing that, whatever the pother may be, it involves grave questions of right and wrong, of crime and punishment, and, no matter how much we enjoy the poetry, we cannot avoid being in some degree disturbed and troubled by it. Now this is surely the effect which Coleridge wished to produce . . . The poem is a myth of a guilty soul and marks in clear stages the passage from crime through punishment to such redemption as is possible in this world."

THE ANNOTATED ANCIENT MARINER

Robert Penn Warren, a poet as well as a distinguished novelist and critic, also defends the religious theme in his essay on *The Ancient Mariner*, "A Poem of Pure Imagination: An Experiment in Reading." (The essay first appeared in an edition of the ballad illustrated by Alexander Calder—see the Foreword—but has since been reprinted, with revisions and additional notes, in Warren's *Selected Essays*.) It is the most influential analysis of *The Ancient Mariner* to have appeared in recent decades. Warren finds *two* metaphorical levels. The most obvious is the one we have been discussing; Warren calls it the theme of "sacramental vision" or "One life," thus emphasizing that the rebirth motif is linked with a vision of nature in which all living things are regarded as worthy of love. The secondary theme Warren calls the theme of the imagination. On this level the killing of the albatross is symbolic of a poet's crime against his imagination, for which he suffers a loss of creative power. I will not discuss this second theme because it would snare us in the complex topic of Coleridge's theory of imagination as distinct from fancy, and also because this aspect of Warren's essay has not met with general acceptance. His defense of Coleridge's primary theme, essentially the rebirth archetype of Maud Bodkin's analysis, is vigorous and carefully reasoned; his defense of the secondary theme is less convincing. For one thing, it involves an interpretation of the moon as a symbol of the imagination and the sun as a symbol of what Coleridge later called, under Kant's influence, the "understanding." Warren follows Kenneth Burke and George Herbert Clarke in regarding the moon as beneficent and the sun as malevolent; unfortunately, considerable mental gymnastics are required to explain such events as two hundred men falling dead under the moon (Part III) and the "sweet jargoning" of the angels under the sun (Part V).

Warren is considered a "New Critic"—a member of that loosely united group of writers who reacted against the Marxist political approach to literature during the thirties by directing attention back to the structure and intrinsic values of the work of art itself. Among detractors of this school, Warren's interpretation of *The Ancient Mariner* is a choice example of how easily New Critical enthusiasm for symbol hunting can lead one down dubious roads. The most vitriolic attack on Warren is Elder Olson's "Symbolic Reading of the Ancient Mariner." (It first appeared in a journal in 1948, was reprinted in *Critics and Criticism,* edited by Ronald S. Crane, and is now most accessible in *Visions and Revisions in Modern American Literary Criticism,* a paperback edited by Bernard S. Oldsey and Arthur O. Lewis, Jr.)

Olson, a poet and professor, belongs to the so-called Chicago School of criticism. This curious group, led by Crane and inspired by Aristotle and Richard P. McKeon, flourished in the forties at the University of Chicago where its members developed a fairly elaborate program for criticism. It was not so much a new theory as an eclectic approach; it accepted all critical methods as legitimate, but emphasized the need for an historical perspective and a special vocabulary, deriving from Aristotle, which the group believed to be more efficient than the vocabularies of rival schools. For some odd reason, however, when a member of the Chicago School actually practices criticism, he sounds just like any other critic, except for a more peevish tone and a stronger emphasis on the imbecility of anyone who disagrees with him. Olson has little use for either of Warren's themes, though he concentrates his fire on the secondary one, finding it compounded of "generous assumptions, undistributed middles, inconsistencies, misinterpretations, ignorationes elenchi, post hoc ergo propter hoc's, etc." That is supposed to take care of Warren, and also let one know that Olson has read Aristotle's discussion of logical fallacies.

Olson is so eager to defend the view that the primary end of a poem is to give "pleasure," that he appends an incredible footnote in which he says it is absurd to suppose an imitative poem *can* have a theme or meaning. "The words have a meaning," he writes; "they mean the poem; but why should the poem itself have any further meaning? What sense is there in asking about the meaning of something which is itself a meaning?" But hierarchies of meaning are commonplace. Marks on paper symbolize the word "stone," and the word "stone" symbolizes a small piece of rock. In the proverb, "A rolling stone gathers no moss," this bit of rock in turn symbolizes a person who drifts from place to place. Olson would no doubt reply that the sum of all such meanings is the proverb itself: therefore it is senseless to seek for a further meaning. Fair enough, but of course Warren can say exactly the same thing about a poem if "poem" is taken in this wide sense. One cannot say Olson is wrong, but only that his terminology—at least in the footnote we are considering—departs so widely from common critical usage that needless confusion results.

There is, it seems to me, much less linguistic obfuscation if one accepts the utterly ordinary view that a narrative poem can have both literal and metaphorical levels of meaning. It is one thing to say that Coleridge did not intend a metaphorical level for his poem—that's a question to be decided by whatever evidence is available—but something else again to argue that the writer of a narrative poem cannot or should not consciously shape his story into a myth. For the right sort of reader, a metaphysical level of meaning can arouse as much "pleasure" as the imitative spectacle of a man experiencing fortunes and misfortunes. A narrative poem, like a person, can be a source of multiple pleasures; the metaphorical level no more weakens the pleasure aroused by the story itself, on its literal level, than a woman's intelligence makes her features less beautiful. Even when a poet's first intent is to arouse the kind of pleasure that derives from what the Chicago School persists in calling the "imitative" aspect of a poem, there is no reason why the poet cannot have all sorts of secondary motives, including the sale of the poem for money and the rhetorical motive of wishing to convert his readers to a certain point of view.

This brings us to a final question, and one that has troubled critics for more than a century and a half: Exactly what is the "moral" of *The Ancient Mariner?* Before trying to answer, we must first glance at the one document that bears most directly on the problem. In *Specimens of the Table Talk of the Late Samuel Taylor Coleridge,* as remembered by his nephew and son-in-law, Henry Nelson Coleridge, the following puzzling conversation occurs (May 31, 1830):

> "Mrs. Barbauld once told me that she admired the *Ancient Mariner* very much, but that there were two faults in it—it was improbable, and had no moral. As for the probability, I owned that that might admit some question; but as to the want of a moral, I told her that in my own judgment the poem had too much; and that the only, or chief, fault, if I might say so, was the obtrusion of the moral sentiment so openly on the reader as a principle or cause of action in a work of such pure imagination. It ought to have had no more moral than the *Arabian Nights* tale of the merchant's sitting down to eat dates by the side of a well, and throwing the shells aside, and lo! a genie starts up, and says he *must* kill the aforesaid merchant *because* one of the date-shells had, it seems, put out the eye of the genie's son."[1]

The passage casts little light on the problem. First, we cannot be sure the conversation is recalled correctly. Assuming it is, we cannot be sure Coleridge was not pulling Mrs. Barbauld's leg. (Anna Letitia

[1]. A summary of the plot of the *Arabian Nights* tale (in which, by the way, the date-shell or pit actually *kills* the genie's son) will be found in Humphry House's *Coleridge,* pp. 90-91, together with some observations on the tale's "moral" theme, without which, House argues, there would be no story.

Interpretations

Barbauld was a popular poet, author, and writer of children's books; she was a devout Presbyterian, much given to pious, humorless moralizing.) Finally, assuming Coleridge did make these remarks and make them seriously, we cannot be sure just what he meant by them. By "moral," did he mean that quatrain "He prayeth best . . .," or was he referring to the theme of crime and punishment that is the framework of the poem? Perhaps he misunderstood Mrs. Barbauld. Did she have one meaning of "moral" in mind and he another? It is amusing to read the conflicting ways in which critics have interpreted Coleridge's comment. The interpretation is always, of course, in support of the critic's way of viewing the poem. Those who find the religious theme either not there or of little significance, cite Coleridge's remarks to Mrs. Barbauld in support of their view. The same passage is just as frequently cited by defenders of the religious theme, for did not the poet admit that there was "too much" of a moral in his ballad? The passage is too ambiguous to decide the matter. We will say no more about it.

There is no doubt, of course, that the poem closes with an explicitly stated "moral" in the "He prayeth best . . ." stanza. On the literal level, it makes an obvious point. The Mariner's woes were brought about by his cruel killing of a bird. Had he loved the bird and not killed it, his shipmates would still be alive and he himself would not be doomed to wander about in a state of life-in-death, still doing penance for his crime. The moral tag is in keeping with the medieval atmosphere of the ballad, and Coleridge made no attempt to remove it from later printings. What are we to make of it?

What we make of it depends on whether we accept the symbolic religious theme. If we insist on reading the poem only on its literal level, we are likely to agree with Irving Babbitt (in an essay on Coleridge in *On Being Creative and Other Essays,* 1932), that the moral is something of a sham. There is, first of all, too "grotesque a disproportion between the mariner's initial act and its consequences." There is no serious ethical theme in the ballad, says Babbitt, "except perhaps a warning as to the fate of the innocent bystander; unless, indeed, one holds that it is fitting that, for having sympathized with the man who shot the albatross, 'four times fifty living men' should perish in torments unspeakable." And how is the Mariner relieved of this awful guilt? "By admiring the color of water snakes." Like Lamb, Babbitt dislikes all the miraculous elements of the poem. He sees them as the product of an abnormal mind, unduly preoccupied with the weird. It differs only in degree from one of Poe's horror tales, and claims a "religious seriousness that at bottom it does not possess."

Lowes likewise finds that the moral, taken out of the poem's context, is untenable. "The punishment," he says, "measured by the standards of a world of balanced penalties, palpably does not fit the crime. But the sphere of balanced penalties is not the given world in which the poem moves. Within *that* world, where birds have tutelary daemons and ships are driven by spectral and angelic powers, consequence and antecedent are in keeping . . ."

Yes, of course. If the poem is no more than a fantasy narrative, like an *Arabian Nights* tale, there is no reason why the Mariner should not warn his listener of the dangers of being cruel to birds. But from this viewpoint it is hard to escape Babbitt's feeling that the great nightmare voyage is finally climaxed by an utterly trivial piece of moralizing.

For the reader who is not repelled by the symbolic religious theme, the moral quatrain need no more be taken in such a literal, trivial sense than we need take the moral of *Moby Dick* to be: It is not good to make one's ultimate concern in life the killing of one particular whale. At the time Coleridge wrote his ballad he was deeply impressed by the sacramental view of nature as he found it in Hartley, and in conversations with Wordsworth who in turn had been influenced by Hartley. The concept that Albert Schweitzer calls "reverence for life" (note that "reverence to all things that God made and loveth" appears in the ballad's gloss) is expressed in other early poems by Coleridge. "The Raven," which Coleridge wrote in the same year that he wrote *The Ancient Mariner,* is in some ways, as Warren reminds us, a crude parallel of the ballad. And countless critics have pointed out that the "He loveth best . . ." quatrain is surely a paraphrase of the following lines from Coleridge's "Religious Musings," written three years before the ballad:

> There is one Mind, one omnipresent Mind,
> Omnific. His most holy name is Love.
> Truth of subliming import! with the which
> Who feeds and saturates his constant soul,
> He from his small particular orbit flies
> With blest outstarting! From himself he flies,
> Stands in the sun, and with no partial gaze
> Views all creation; and he loves it all,
> And blesses it, and calls it very good!

If we are entitled to view the shooting of the albatross as a prototype of sin against God, we are entitled to interpret the word "small" in the moral quatrain as more than just a reference to birds and water snakes, or the admonition that if one slaps a mosquito one should feel at least a twinge of remorse. The moral surely is—and it matters not a rap whether Coleridge did or did not consciously intend it this way—one best loves God by loving his fellow man. "God be praised for all things!" he closed a letter in 1796, the year before he started his ballad. "A faith in goodness makes all nature good." Two weeks before he died, aware that he did not have long to live, Coleridge expressed regret that he would be unable to finish the systematic philosophy he had long hoped to write, and added: "For, as God hears me, the originating, continuing and sustaining wish and design in my heart were to exalt the glory of His name; and, which is the same thing in other words, to promote the improvement of mankind. But *visum aliter Deo,* and 'His Will be done!'"

Need I remind some readers that it was Jesus who said that on two commandments hang all the Laws and Prophets? "Thou shalt love the Lord thy God with all thy heart, and with all thy soul, and with all thy mind, and with all thy strength: this is the first commandment. And the second is like, namely this, Thou shalt love thy neighbor as thyself. There is none other commandment greater than these." (Mark 12:30,31.) In Coleridge's ballad this moral may have a jingly, Sunday school sound, as well as grotesque associations with albatrosses and water snakes, but there is no reason why we should not take it, on the higher mythic level of the poem, in the widest sense.

Many critics have defended the simplicity and naïveté of the ballad's moral quatrain, but none more effectively than Mrs. Margaret Oliphant. In her *Literary History of England,* 1882 (Vol. I, Chap. 7, "The Lyrical Ballads"), she writes: "And then comes the ineffable, half-childish, half-divine simplicity of those soft moralizings at the end, so strangely different from the tenor of the tale, so wonderfully perfecting its visionary strain. After all, the poet seems to say, after this weird excursion into the very deepest, awful heart of the seas and mysteries, here is your child's moral, a tender little half-trivial sentiment, yet profound as the blue depths of heaven:

> He prayeth best, who loveth best
> All things both great and small;
> For the dear God who loveth us,
> He made and loveth all.

"This unexpected gentle conclusion brings our feet back to the common soil with a bewildered sweetness of relief and soft quiet after the prodigious strain of mental excitement which is like nothing else we can remember in poetry. The effect is one rarely produced, and which few poets have the strength and daring to accomplish, sinking from the highest notes of spiritual music to the absolute simplicity of exhausted nature."

At present, Christian churches in this country are suddenly discovering the moral's application to the racially "small" in our midst, our Negro minority. "He prayeth best who loveth best . . ." How fare, one wonders, the prayers of our southern Catholics and Protestants who refuse to take communion if the person next to them has skin of a different color? Cross-bows come in all shapes and sizes.

I should like to end my remarks with an ambiguous fable of my own, or rather, a fable I discovered in *The New York Times,* Sunday, February 2, 1964. According to the *Times,* and later news releases from the National Audubon Society, the U.S. Navy had found it necessary to destroy about 20,000 of an estimated 150,000 albatrosses that nest on Sand and Eastern islands, part of the Midway group in the Hawaiian archipelago.

Two species of albatross—the Laysan and the Blackfooted albatrosses —build nests on the island. The huge birds have a habit of getting in the way of Navy planes when the planes take off. No Navy personnel had yet been killed, but many planes had been damaged by colliding with the birds. One plane had its radar equipment and three rudders knocked off. Every hour and a half a giant plane takes off, with twenty-two men and six million dollars worth of electronic equipment. Every hour and a half a plane lands. The flights are part of the country's early-warning radar network.

The Navy had tried various measures. It set off flares, mortar shells, and bazookas. It shouted at the birds through loudspeakers. It hoisted scarecrows. The friendly gooney birds (as they are called by the local sailors) seemed to enjoy watching these antics. The Navy destroyed the nests. The goonies made new ones. Finally, more drastic steps had to be taken. The birds show no fear of man, so it was easy to capture them, put them in sealed chambers, and kill them with carbon monoxide from Navy truck exhausts. Quite apart from all this, about one hundred albatrosses are killed each week by flying into a huge antenna of guy wires on Eastern Island.

Carl W. Buchheister, president of the National Audubon Society, had just returned from Midway where he had gone to investigate the situation. He recommended hiring a full-time resident ornithologist, continuing research on ways of keeping the birds off the airstrips, and flagging the guy wires. The Navy, he reported, shared his "extreme regret" that their "elimination program had become necessary."

PART   V

Selected References

THE WRITINGS OF COLERIDGE

Books published in his lifetime:

Poems on Various Subjects, 1796.

Lyrical Ballads, 1798.   Currently available as a Doubleday Dolphin paperback (no date). A hardcover edition edited with introduction, notes, and appendices by R. L. Brett and A. R. Jones was published by Barnes and Noble, 1963.

The second edition of *Lyrical Ballads,* with a famous preface added by Wordsworth, appeared in 1800. Coleridge had acquiesced to demands of Wordsworth and others that the archaic words of his ballad be modernized, so there were many changes in the poem's text. In the 1802 and 1805 editions of *Lyrical Ballads,* textual changes were slight. The marginal glosses were not printed until 1817, when Coleridge included the ballad in his *Sibylline Leaves.*

A Statesman's Manual; or the Bible the Best Guide for Political Skill and Foresight, 1816.

Biographia Literaria, 1817. Edited by H. N. Coleridge and Sara Coleridge, 1847. Edited by J. Shawcross, 1907.

A Lay Sermon, 1817.

Sibylline Leaves, 1817. Currently available as a Doubleday Dolphin paperback (no date).

Lectures on Shakespeare, 1818.

The Friend: A Series of Essays in Three Volumes, 1818. Edited by H. N. Coleridge, 1837.

Aids to Reflection in the Formation of a Manly Character, on the Several Grounds of Prudence, Morality, and Religion, 1825.

Poetical Works, 1828.

On the Constitution of Church and State, According to the Idea of Each; with Aids Toward a Right Judgment on the Late Catholic Bill, 1830.

Posthumous prose works and collections:

Specimens of the Table Talk of Samuel Taylor Coleridge, edited by H. N. Coleridge, 1835. *The Table Talk and Omnia of Samuel Taylor Coleridge,* edited by T. Ashe, 1884.

The Literary Remains of Samuel Taylor Coleridge, edited by H. N. Coleridge, 1836–39.

Confessions of an Inquiring Spirit; Letters on the inspiration of scriptures, edited by H. N. Coleridge, 1840. Edited by H. St.J. Hart, 1956.

Essays on His Own Times, edited by Sara Coleridge, 1850.

Notes on the English Divines, edited by Derwent Coleridge, 1853.

Notes, Theological, Political, and Miscellaneous, edited by Derwent Coleridge, 1853.

The Complete Works of Samuel Taylor Coleridge, 7 volumes, edited by W. G. T. Shedd, 1853–54.

Miscellanies, Aesthetic and Literary, to which is added "The Theory of Life," edited by T. Ashe, 1885.

Anima Poetae, from the unpublished notebooks of S. T. Coleridge, edited by E. H. Coleridge, 1895.

Biographia Epistolaris, Being the Biographical Supplement of Coleridge's Biographia Literaria, *with Additional Letters, etc.,* edited by A. Turnbull, 1911.

Coleridge on Logic and Learning, edited by Alice D. Snyder, 1929.

Coleridge's Shakespearean Criticism, edited by Thomas M. Raysor, 1930.

Coleridge's Miscellaneous Criticism, edited by Thomas M. Raysor, 1936.

The Philosophical Lectures, Hitherto Unpublished, of Samuel Taylor Coleridge, edited by Kathleen Coburn, 1949.

The Portable Coleridge, edited by I. A. Richards, 1950. Viking paperback, 1961.

Inquiring Spirit, a New Presentation of Coleridge from His Published and Unpublished Prose Writings, edited by Kathleen Coburn, 1951.

Posthumous collections of poetry:

The Poetical Works of Samuel Taylor Coleridge, edited by James Dykes Campbell, 1893.

The Complete Poetical Works of Samuel Taylor Coleridge, edited by Ernest Hartley Coleridge, 1912.

The Poems of Samuel Taylor Coleridge, edited by Ernest Hartley Coleridge, 1912. Same as preceding book, without the dramas. Currently available as an Oxford paperback, 1961.

Selected References

Notebooks and letters:

The Notebooks of Samuel Taylor Coleridge, Vol. I: 1794–1804, Vol. II: 1804–8, edited by Kathleen Coburn, 1957–61. First two volumes of a projected five-volume edition of Coleridge's notebooks.

Letters of Samuel Taylor Coleridge, edited by Ernest Hartley Coleridge, 1895.

Unpublished Letters of Samuel Taylor Coleridge, edited by Earl Leslie Griggs, 1932.

Collected Letters of Samuel Taylor Coleridge, edited by Earl Leslie Griggs, 1956–59. Four of six projected volumes have been issued.

Books on the Life of Coleridge

Joseph Cottle, *Early Recollections, chiefly relating to the late Samuel Taylor Coleridge, during his long residence in Bristol,* 1837.

James Gillman, *The Life of Samuel Taylor Coleridge,* 1838. The first biography, by the poet's friend and physician.

Joseph Cottle, *Reminiscences of Samuel Taylor Coleridge and Robert Southey,* 1847.

Henry Duff Traill, *Coleridge,* 1884.

Hall Caine, *Life of Samuel Taylor Coleridge,* 1887.

James Dykes Campbell, *Samuel Taylor Coleridge: A narrative of the events of his life,* 1894.

Richard Garnett, *Coleridge,* 1904.

William Knight, *Coleridge and Wordsworth in the West Country,* 1913.

Lucy Watson, *Coleridge at Highgate,* 1925.

Hugh I'Anson Fausset, *Samuel Taylor Coleridge,* 1926.

John Charpentier, *Coleridge, the Sublime Somnambulist,* translated from the French by M. V. Nugent, 1929.

Meyer H. Abrams, *The Milk of Paradise,* 1934. On the influence of opium on Coleridge.

Stephen Potter, *Coleridge and STC,* 1935.

Edmund Kerchever Chambers, *Samuel Taylor Coleridge: A biographical study,* 1938.

Lawrence Hanson, *The Life of Samuel Taylor Coleridge: The early years,* 1938.

Francis Winwar, *Farewell the Banner,* 1938. On Wordsworth, Coleridge, and Dorothy Wordsworth. Reproduces (p. 322) Max Beerbohm's caricature of Coleridge "table-talking" to sleeping guests.

Earl Leslie Griggs, *Coleridge Fille: A Biography of Sara Coleridge,* 1940. Although about Coleridge's daughter, the book gives a vivid picture of the poet's troubled domestic life.

Richard W. Armour and Raymond F. Howes, *Coleridge the Talker,* 1940. An anthology of accounts of Coleridge by his contemporaries.

Laura Benet, *Coleridge: Poet of Wild Enchantment,* 1952.

Herscher M. Margoliouth, *Wordsworth and Coleridge, 1795–1834,* 1953.

Elisabeth Schneider, *Coleridge, Opium, and Kubla Khan,* 1953.

Maurice Carpenter, *The Indifferent Horseman: The Divine Comedy of Samuel Taylor Coleridge,* 1954.

George Whalley, *Coleridge and Sara Hutchinson and the Asra Poems,* 1955.

Books on Coleridge's Views and Writings

Joseph Henry Green, *Spiritual Philosophy Founded on the Teaching of the Late Samuel Taylor Coleridge,* 1865.

John Livingston Lowes, *The Road to Xanadu,* 1927. Vintage Books (paperback), 1959. *The* classic, indispensable study of the sources of *The Ancient Mariner* and *Kubla Khan.*

John H. Muirhead, *Coleridge as Philosopher,* 1930.

Edmund Blunden and Earl Leslie Griggs (editors), *Coleridge: Studies by Several Hands,* 1934.

Ivor Armstrong Richards, *Coleridge on Imagination,* 1934. Indiana University (paperback), 1960.

Margaret Sherwood, *Coleridge's Imaginative Concept of Imagination,* 1937.

Arthur H. Nethercot, *The Road to Tryermaine,* 1939. A study of the sources of *Christabel.*

Charles R. Sanders, *Coleridge and the Broad Church Movement,* 1942.

Herbert Read, *Coleridge as Critic,* 1949.

Humphry House, *Coleridge: The Clark Lectures, 1951–52,* 1953.

James V. Baker, *The Sacred River: Coleridge's Theory of the Imagination,* 1957.

J. B. Beer, *Coleridge the Visionary,* 1959. Collier Books (paperback), 1962.

John A. Colmer, *Coleridge: Critic of Society,* 1959.

Marshall Suther, *The Dark Night of Samuel Taylor Coleridge,* 1960.

James D. Boulger, *Coleridge as Religious Thinker,* 1961.

Carl R. Woodring, *Politics in the Poetry of Coleridge,* 1961.

Selected References

Royal A. Gettmann (editor), *The Rime of the Ancient Mariner: A Handbook,* 1961. A valuable paperback anthology of 31 selections from various authors discussing the ballad, together with the poem's 1798 and 1834 versions.

Richard Harter Fogle, *The Idea of Coleridge's Criticism,* 1962.

Max F. Schulz, *The Poetic Voices of Coleridge,* 1963.

Editions of The Ancient Mariner

No attempt is made here to list the many hundreds of collections of Coleridge's poetry and special editions of *The Rime of the Ancient Mariner,* many of which contain brief annotations of the ballad. From 1890 to 1930 scores of small editions of the poem, annotated by diverse hands, were published for school use in the United States and England. The interested reader will find most of these volumes listed in *Samuel Taylor Coleridge: A Selected Bibliography,* 1935, edited by Virginia Wadlow Kennedy and Mary Neill Barton. The following list includes only volumes that, for one reason or another, seem to me of special interest.

Annotated editions:

Coleridge's Ancient Mariner, edited by Katherine Lee Bates, 1889.

Three Narrative Poems, edited by George A. Watrous, 1898.

The Ancient Mariner, Kubla Khan, Christabel, edited by Tuley F. Huntington, 1898. Revised by H. Y. Moffett, 1929.

The Ancient Mariner, edited by Pelham Edgar, 1900.

The Rime of the Ancient Mariner, Christabel, and Other Poems, edited by Julian W. Abernethy, 1907.

The Rime of the Ancient Mariner and The Vision of Sir Launfal, edited by William Vaughn Moody, 1906.

Illustrated editions:

Edinburgh: Alexander Hill, 1837. Illustrated by David Scott.

London: Sampson Low, 1858. Illustrated by Birket Foster and others.

London: Art-Union, 1863. Illustrated by J. Noel Paton.

London: Doré Gallery, 1875. Illustrated by Gustave Doré. First U.S. edition, Harpers, 1876.

London: Gay and Bird, 1900. Illustrated by Herbert Cole.

New York: Dodge, 1903. Illustrated by Lolita Perine.

London: T. C. and E. C. Jack, 1906. Illustrated by Paul Woodroffe.

London: G. G. Harrap, 1910. Illustrated by Willy Pogány.

Paris: 1921. Translated by Alfred Jarry. Illustrated by A. Deslignères.

Yellow Springs, Ohio: Kahoe and Spieth, 1927. Illustrated by Gustav Uhlmann.

Bristol: Douglas Cleverdon, 1929. Illustrated by David Jones.

New York: Macmillan, 1929. Illustrated by A. Gladys Peck.

New York: Cheshire House, 1931. Illustrated by H. Charles Tomlinson. Introduction by Edmund Blunden.

London: L. C. C. Central School of Arts and Crafts, 1937. Illustrated by Ellaline Davies.

New York: Heritage, 1938. Illustrated by Gordon Grant.

Mount Vernon, N. Y.: Peter Pauper Press, 1939. Illustrated by Paul McPharlin.

London: Chatto and Windus, 1943. Illustrated by Mervyn Peake.

New York: Limited Editions Club, 1945. Illustrated and hand-colored by Edward A. Wilson. The introduction by John Livingston Lowes is a reprint of Chapter 16 of *The Road to Xanadu*.

New York: Reynal and Hitchcock, 1946. Illustrated by Alexander Calder. Contains the first printing of Robert Penn Warren's well-known essay.

Books Containing Essays and References of Special Interest on Coleridge and The Ancient Mariner

Thomas Carlyle, *Life of John Sterling*, 1851. Contains Carlyle's well-known account of his visit with Coleridge at Highgate.

Algernon Charles Swinburne, "Coleridge," in *Essays and Studies*, 1876.

Thomas De Quincey, "Coleridge," and "Southey, Wordsworth, and Coleridge." The most accessible volume containing these essays is the Everyman's Library edition of De Quincey's *Reminiscences of the English Lake Poets*, 1907.

Walter Pater, "Coleridge," in *Appreciations*, 1889.

Sir Leslie Stephen, "Coleridge," in *Hours in a Library*, Vol. III, 1892.

Solomon Francis Gingerich, "Coleridge," in *Essays in the Romantic Poets*, 1924.

Selected References

George McLean Harper, "Coleridge's Conversation Poems," in *Spirit of Delight*, 1928.

Irving Babbitt, "Coleridge and Imagination," in *On Being Creative and Other Essays*, 1932. Famous attack on the "sham moral" of the ballad.

Maud Bodkin, "A Study of 'The Ancient Mariner' and of the Rebirth Archetype," in *Archetypal Patterns in Poetry*, 1934. Oxford (paperback), 1963.

Robert Cecil Bald, "Coleridge and 'The Ancient Mariner': Addenda to *The Road to Xanadu*," in *Nineteenth Century Studies*, edited by Herbert Davis, William DeVane, and Bald, 1940.

Kenneth Burke, *The Philosophy of Literary Form*, 1941. Vintage Books (paperback), 1957. See index for many references to *The Ancient Mariner*.

George Wilson Knight, "Coleridge's Divine Comedy," in *The Starlit Dome*, 1942. Revised, 1960.

Newton P. Stallknecht, "The Moral of The Ancient Mariner," in *Strange Seas of Thought*, 1945. Revised, 1958.

Ernest De Selincourt, "Coleridge's *Dejection: an Ode*," in *Wordsworthian and Other Studies*, 1947.

Eustace M. W. Tillyard, "The Rime of the Ancient Mariner," in *Five Poems, 1470–1870*, 1948.

Cecil M. Bowra, "The Ancient Mariner," in *The Romantic Imagination*, 1949. Galaxy Books (paperback), 1961.

Ivor Armstrong Richards, "Introduction," in *The Portable Coleridge*, 1950. Viking (paperback), 1961.

Lane Cooper, "The Power of the Eye in Coleridge," in *Late Harvest*, 1952. A reprinting of a 1910 paper.

Thomas M. Raysor, "Coleridge," and Rene Wellek, "Coleridge's Philosophy and Criticism," in *The English Romantic Poets*, edited by Raysor, revised 1956.

Robert Penn Warren, "A Poem of Pure Imagination: An Experiment in Reading," in *Selected Essays*, 1958. A reprinting, with revisions, of Warren's influential 1946 essay.

Raymond L. Brett, "Coleridge's *The Rime of the Ancient Mariner*," in *Reason and Imagination*, 1960.

Elder Olson, "A Symbolic Reading of the 'Ancient Mariner,'" in *Visions and Revisions in Modern American Literary Criticism*, edited by Bernard S. Oldsey and Arthur C. Lewis, Jr., Dutton (paperback), 1962. A reprinting of Olson's vitriolic 1948 attack on Robert Penn Warren's interpretation of the ballad.

Magazine Articles on The Ancient Mariner

The following check list, selected from many hundreds of periodical references, does not include articles later reprinted in a book listed in the preceding section.

Gertrude Garrogues, "Coleridge's Ancient Mariner," *Journal of Speculative Philosophy*, Vol. XIV (July, 1880), 327–38. The ballad is analyzed as a detailed allegory of Christian sin and redemption.

Norman Guthrie, "The Rime of the Ancient Mariner as Prophecy," *Sewanee Review*, VI (1898), 200–13. Defends the religious theme, and the moral stanza as the "very germ of the whole poem."

Charles Wharton Stork, "The Influence of the Popular Ballad on Wordsworth and Coleridge," *Publications of the Modern Language Association*, XXIX (1914), 299–326.

Ernest Hartley Coleridge, "The Genesis of the Ancient Mariner," *Poetry Review*, IX (1918), 271–77.

Thomas M. Raysor, "Coleridge and 'Asra,'" *Studies in Philology*, XXVI (July, 1929). Basic reference on the poet's relationship with Sara Hutchinson.

B. R. McElderry, Jr., "Coleridge's Revisions of The Ancient Mariner," *North Carolina University Studies in Philology*, XXIX (January, 1932), 68–94.

George Herbert Clarke, "Certain Symbols in The Ancient Mariner," *Queen's Quarterly*, XL (February, 1933), 27–45. A symbolic approach to the religious theme.

Elizabeth Nitchie, "The Moral of The Ancient Mariner Reconsidered," *Publications of the Modern Language Association*, XLVIII (September, 1933), 867–76. A defense of the ballad's moral stanza.

H. W. Garrod, "The Mystery of The Ancient Mariner," *Poetry Review* (July-August. 1934), 269–76.

Dorothy Waples, "David Hartley in The Ancient Mariner," *Journal of English and Germanic Philology*, XXXV (July, 1936), 337–51. Traces the influence of Hartley's philosophy on the ballad.

Eugene Marius Bewley, "The Poetry of Coleridge," *Scrutiny*, VIII (March, 1940), 406–20. Defends the view that the Christian theme is the core of the ballad, but in a disguised, fragmented way; caricatured and debased by the supernatural machinery.

D. W. Harding, "The Theme of the Ancient Mariner," *Scrutiny*, IX (March, 1941), 334–42. Defends the religious theme.

Selected References

George Whalley, "The Mariner and the Albatross," *The University of Toronto Quarterly*, XVI (July, 1947), 381–98. Views the albatross as a symbol of Coleridge's creative imagination.

Elmer Edgar Stoll, "Symbolism in Coleridge," *Publications of the Modern Language Association*, LXIII (March, 1948), 214–33. An attack on Robert Penn Warren's symbolic approach.

Lionel Stevenson, "The Ancient Mariner as a Dramatic Monolog," *The Personalist*, XXX (January, 1949), 34–44. Argues against the religious theme; the poem is merely a dramatic story about a superstitious sailor who thinks that killing a bird has caused his woes.

Coleman O. Parsons, "The Mariner and the Albatross," *Virginia Quarterly Review*, XXVI (Winter, 1950), 102–23. Defense of the religious theme.

David Beres, "A Dream, a Vision, and a Poem," *The International Journal of Psycho-Analysis*, XXXII, Part 2 (1951), 97–116.

Tristram P. Coffin, "Coleridge's Use of the Ballad Stanza in the Rime of the Ancient Mariner," *Modern Language Quarterly*, XII (December, 1951), 437–45.

Maren-Sofie Rostvig, "Another Source for Some Stanzas of the Rime of the Ancient Mariner," *Modern Language Notes*, LXVI (December, 1951), 543–46. Suggests that the source of "A sail, a sail," and "Hark, hark," in the ballad's first version may be a poem by Charles Cotton.

Thomas M. Raysor, "Coleridge's Comment on the Moral of The Ancient Mariner," *Philological Quarterly*, XXXI (January, 1952), 88–91.

Newell F. Ford, "Kenneth Burke and Robert Penn Warren: Criticism by Obsessive Metaphor," *Journal of English and Germanic Philology*, LIII (April, 1954), 172–77. An attack on the symbolic approach.

A. A. Mendilow, "Symbolism in Coleridge and the Dantesque Element in The Ancient Mariner," *Scripta Hierosolymitana*, II (1955), 25–81. The ballad is viewed as a rebirth myth lapsing occasionally into allegory. The influence of Dante is stressed.

Richard Harter Fogle, "The Genre of The Ancient Mariner," *Tulane Studies in English*, VII (1957), 111–24. Stresses the "one life" theme.

Karl Kroeber, "The Rime of the Ancient Mariner as Stylized Epic," *Transactions of the Wisconsin Academy of Sciences, Arts and Letters*, XLVI (1957), 179–87. Argues that the ballad is a quest epic similar to the Odyssey.

J. W. R. Purser, "Interpretation of the Ancient Mariner," *Review of English Studies*, New Series, VIII (August, 1957), 249–56. Defends the religious theme.

Davis Beres, "The Notebooks of Samuel Taylor Coleridge," *The Psychoanalytic Quarterly,* XXVIII (1959), 267–70. A review of the first two parts of volume one of Coleridge's notebooks, edited by Kathleen Coburn.

Elliott B. Gose, Jr., "Coleridge and the Luminous Gloom," *Publications of the Modern Language Association,* LXXV (June, 1960), 238–44. Symbolic approach to the religious theme.

Malcolm Ware, "The Rime of the Ancient Mariner: A Discourse on Prayer," *Review of English Studies,* New Series, XI (August, 1960), 303–4. Defends the religious theme, with special emphasis on the poem's references to prayer.

Malcolm Ware, "Coleridge's 'Spectre-Bark': A Slave Ship?" *Philological Quarterly,* XL (October, 1961), 589–93. Suggests that the poem's spectre ship may have been intended as a slave ship.

Books on Gustave Doré

Life and Reminiscences of Gustave Doré, Blanche Macchetta, 1885.

Masterpieces from the Works of Gustave Doré, introduction by Charlotte Adams, 1887.

Life of Gustave Doré, W. Blanchard Jerrold, 1891.

The Terrible Gustave Doré, Hellmut Lehmann-Haupt, 1943.

Gustave Doré, Millicent Rose, 1946.